ROMAN
PROVINCIAL
ADMINISTRATION

D0317530

ROMAN
PROVINCIAL
ADMINISTRATION

JOHN ROGAN

AMBERLEY

To D.M.R. for constant support

First published 2011

Amberley Publishing
Cirencester Road, Chalford,
Stroud, Gloucestershire, GL6 8PE

www.amberleybooks.com

Copyright © John Rogan 2011

The right of John Rogan to be identified as the Author
of this work has been asserted in accordance with the
Copyrights, Designs and Patents Act 1988.

British Library Cataloguing in Publication Data.
A catalogue record for this book is available from the British Library.

ISBN 978-1-4456-0179-3

Typeset in 10pt on 12pt Sabon.
Typesetting and Origination by Amberley Publishing.
Printed in Great Britain.

CONTENTS

Romans, never forget that government is your medium. Be this your art: to practise men in the habits of peace; generosity to the conquered and firmness against aggressors.

Virgil

The sagacious reader who is capable of reading between these lines to perceive what is not written but implied will be able to reach some conclusions.

Goethe

ACKNOWLEDGEMENTS

I should like to acknowledge the kindness of Chris Wiles in making his photographs and additional material so freely available to me; the shrewdness of Jean Lawrence in her clerical work: she has been a vigilant sub-editor; the charity of former students for their candid responses in explorations of this subject; the support and advice of Alan Sutton and Amberley Publishing; and finally the tolerance and interest of my wife and family in excusing the demands made upon them. All of them have been, in one way or another, 'partners in my labours'. Dean Gale, a seventeenth-century scholar, once wrote that there was sociability in such studies. That is true, but the writer must accept accountability for whatever is amiss in the outcome. It is the price of authorship.

John Rogan
August 2010

LIST OF ILLUSTRATIONS
AND DIAGRAMS

1. The boundaries of the Empire set in stone; this reconstruction of the Roman fort of Arbeia at the eastern end of Hadrian's Wall shows the determination of Hadrian to exercise control over his northern frontier.

2. Augustus was the architect of what became the Roman Empire, together with the procedures of provincial administration largely described in this book.

3. The inscription of a consul ordinarius in the Roman Colosseum. The two ordinary consuls took office on 1 January, and the year following was named after them for dating purposes. Resignation might follow after a short time; a replacement was known as a suffectus. The process ensured the supply of ex-consulars capable of taking up senior appointments reserved for that rank.

4. This early third-century inscription from Caerwent shows how an official could move from a senatorial to an imperial province as well as from a military to an administrative command. For more details, see Appendix.

5. Trajan was one of the most successful, militarily, of all the Roman Emperors, pushing the Empire to its limits. This included an area north of the River Danube (almost equivalent to modern Romania)

which became the province of Dacia, for a short time only. The title was used later for a province to the south of the river. As a successful soldier, Trajan was commemorated by his column, which gives a detailed insight into the Roman army of his day.

6. The Arch of Constantine in Rome is an example of the way in which some Emperors chose to mark their triumphs. Governors had to be careful not to interfere with imperial prerogatives, lest their careers be cut short.

7. Inscription on the Arch of Constantine: note the depth of the incisions.

8. Hadrian's Arch in Athens. There were arches of different kinds throughout the Empire, generally celebrating an Emperor.

9. The name on the tombstone of this governor of Pannonia Inferior found at Aquincum (Budapest) has disappeared, but the title of his role is given: 'Leg Aug Pr Pr' (legatus augusti pro praetore). The name of the dedicator is not given, but we are told he/she was happy to discharge this duty of commemoration and did so willingly: 'VSLM' (*votum solvit libens merito*).

10. The statue of Boudicca in her chariot, brandishing her weapons, is a modern one. The leader of a major uprising against the Romans in the first century CE has become the icon for brave Britons resisting the threat of a foreign invader.

11. Cogidubnus. This inscription throws light upon local Roman government. The status of Cogidubnus as a client king is made abundantly clear: note the careful description of all his titles. He is associated with the large building complex at Fishbourne, but the inscription is to be found in the wall of a building in Chichester.

12. The man dressed as a Roman soldier is a reminder of the fact that the security of the Emperor depended upon retaining the support of the army. Later in the third century the army, whether

in the provinces or in Rome itself, became the political power broker. But whatever happened in the capital, the provincial administration remained heavily reliant on military personnel for the exercise of rule.

Diagram 1 Central government and the provinces.
Diagram 2 Imperial provinces.
Diagram 3 Provincial administration.
Diagram 4 Provincial headquarters.
Diagram 5 Legionary command structure.
Diagram 6 Dioceses and the Empire.
Diagram 7 Environment of a role.
Diagram 8 Organisation and the person.

PREFACE

Anyone interested in any aspect of the Roman Empire will find, almost invariably, a variety of studies available. In particular, prosopography has brought to life all sorts and conditions of people from every level of society. It has made possible the elucidation of their careers as well as their family connections. Those who held office provided the governmental structures which helped to hold a variety of local societies together within the Empire as a whole, while at the same time promoting the culture of the *imperium*. When correlated with the study of organisations, we are able, in the present volume, to present a sketch of the main features of that structure, as far as the provinces of the Empire are concerned. Of course one becomes aware of gaps, exceptions and ambiguities; these are inevitable in any historical enterprise, but enough may emerge to display at least the main roles and role relationships within the provincial administration which enabled it to operate. How well it did so is hard to assess. Epigraphy is mostly silent and literary sources may be biased by the unstated presuppositions of the writers. An analysis of career roles, together with what we are told of events, may enable us to make at least a provisional assessment. Thus, one might assume continued usage to demonstrate a utility relevant to the needs of generations of administrators. If reforms take place, we must seek to discover what the conditions which brought about the changes were. As R. G. Collingwood taught, in order to understand an action we must understand the question to which the action was the result.

Thus, what were the objectives of the provincial administration? In what context, and with what resources?

However, judgements ought to be cautious. No one can say infallibly how any organisation, past or present, should be designed. Professor Derek Newman has taught us that 'there is no set of "principles of organisation" that is generally applicable to give predetermined solutions. Such a claim would be refuted by our everyday experience of organisations'. Roman provincial administration was a particular organisation, with its own idiosyncratic features. We have our own contemporary experiences. These may enable light to be thrown upon the Roman, for by comparing the one with the other we may conclude that there are general features common to both. These we can use in our present study. This explains the structure of the chapters which follow: first the nature of roles and role relationships, then the structure of central government as far as the provinces were concerned, followed by a sketch of the values which formed the sinews of both; after this we proceed to a description of the main features of provincial administration, ending with a postscript which hints at its contribution to later organisations.

Finally, the use of some words and phrases may strike the purist as jargon. That may be so, but the writer craves the indulgence of the reader for their employment, reminding us all that if we use Latin terminology in the study of Roman history, we may also use the English vocabulary employed in organisation analysis in this enterprise, inelegant as it may be.

John Rogan

INTRODUCTION

Roman provincial administration during the early centuries of the Common Era can be studied as an organisation whose features may be discerned by means of an analysis derived from concepts which appear to be common to people working in any kind of common enterprise. A parade of characters, describing who they were and what they did, fails to do justice to them or the organisation in which they served. 'The well- or ill-functioning of an institution is not just a matter of "personalities": its primary source lies buried in the structure of the institution itself.' Roles and role relationships are the 'building blocks' out of which an organisation is constructed. As soon as anyone assumes an appointment in an organisation their behaviour changes, to be governed not only by their abilities, important as they may be, but perhaps more importantly by the policies, customs, protocols and practices of the organisation itself. They determine both the tasks to be performed and the way in which they are executed. No governor of Britain, or any other official, had a free rein to do whatever he wanted. There was, indeed, some discretion, as we shall see, but a good deal of his work was prescribed. His personal style would, of course, affect his performance, which was more likely, however, to be assessed by the Emperor and his ministers by the results which were achieved, measured against the terms of reference of his appointment. Roman provincial administration was clearly a bureaucracy, resting upon the authority of the Emperor, in which roles and the relationship between roles were defined and managed.

A role, therefore, is a behaviour pattern largely determined by those who oversee the organisation as a whole, and who have determined the contents of roles and the nature of the relationships between them. Roles are not separate social entities, but parts of role relationships which help to define the roles themselves. A role cannot exist by itself. Furthermore, what is not stated should be considered as important as what is. A governor would find his principal activities were prescribed for him, together with his organisational relationships: for example, it might be judged necessary to set out the governor's relationship with the procurator and his staff, who were also stationed in the province. The boundaries of these roles are important, partly because inevitably they are approximations, to a lesser or greater extent, and partly because they are the frontier where one person interacts with another, with all this entails in human relationships. The role relationship is shaped both by the formal statement made about it and by what those involved assume it to be, to which we should add how everyone finds it actually to operate. A title may not be an accurate description of a role's tasks: a frumentarius was originally an official who was responsible for the collection of corn, but in the course of time Hadrian made them his agents. While apparently discharging a straightforwardly open task, they could be employed as a 'front' for a variety of other, perhaps confidential, imperial purposes. We should seek an accurate role specification, because in this way we may be able to identify those features of roles which should be the proper determinants of behaviour and action. A change of person does not change either the role or its relationships. They are detachable from the occupant. Any changes come about by the action of a higher authority; in the case of high officials this would be the office of the Emperor.

What does vary is the capacity of individuals occupying a role – their ability to carry out successfully the tasks required of them. Here personal characteristics infuse the role, because results depend not merely upon requisite job description and role relationship, but upon inherent ability combined with a willingness to deploy it to the fulfilment of necessary activities. For example, one reason for the structure of governorships in the Empire was the perceived failure of some Republican governors to act appropriately by seeming to prefer to use their term of office for self-aggrandisement.

The fact is that organisations can dehumanise those who work in them, a perception well put by Lord Acton in his aphorism that 'power tends to corrupt and absolute power tends to corrupt absolutely'. Authority is one thing, power is another. The latter is a personal attribute affecting the way in which office holders use or misuse the authority conferred upon them. It is an attribute which gives the holder the right to exercise rewards and punishments on those people over whom power is exercised. The effectiveness of any authority depends on the power of the authoriser. Unless there is the capacity to enforce the required behaviour requisite for the achievement of stated objectives, authority is of no effect. The sources of the necessary power may be status, prestige, psychological dominance or physical force, charisma or what is often called force of character.

As a nineteen-year-old heir of Julius Caesar, Octavianus appeared to lack the power to claim his inheritance. Those who thought so made a serious error of judgement. With his victory in the civil war following the death of Caesar, authority was conferred upon him by the Senate and People of Rome. His longevity helped him and his successors to secure the legitimacy of the principate. Once he held authority, sustained by his power, he could delegate the former to whomsoever he wished, but their effectiveness in post depended upon their personal power, except for one thing: successful performance in a role depends on the provision of adequate resources, of people, money and equipment; they are all significant determinants of success, regardless of the capacity of an office holder. The lack of them can often result in the failure to achieve desired objectives. Honorius' message to the provincial leaders informing them that they should look to their own defence was a statement about the lack of resources available to both the central and provincial government. It has commonly been assumed, at any rate in Britain, that the letter was addressed to the provincial administrators there. However, the recipient could well have been the officials of Bruttium. A scribal error could at some point have been made. It makes little difference; with or without a letter, neither Britain nor Bruttium was going to receive assistance. The resources were not available.

Due weight must be given to personal attitudes, especially in an authoritarian regime like the Empire. They would operate at all levels, but would be crucial in the person of the Emperor. The bizarre behaviour of Caligula and the artistic fantasies of Nero displayed the inadequacies of their personal power, which in turn degraded their authority. The paranoia of Domitian helped to undermine his authority, while Tacitus thought his jealousy prevented the further employment of Agricola after the termination of his governorship of Britain. During this time, however, the inadequacies of the head of state did not seem to threaten the provincial administration: the structure of the *imperium* protected it. Though there may have been rapacious governors or incompetent officials, they could be dealt with by ministers of the central government. The separatist regimes of Albinus and Carausius in Britain did not cause a breakdown in the internal administration or local government. Men were appointed to governmental posts by the decision of the Emperor. They fell from them in the same way. Tenure was at imperial pleasure: there was no security in any appointment. In extreme cases, as with Nero and Seneca, a man's public life could end with a command or, at least, an inescapable hint to commit suicide.

We need not assume that internal reforms were driven by a desire for efficiency; we should look rather for a political motivation. Those we see appear to have been driven by attempts to give the supreme authority greater security; hence the division of provinces, as in Britain and Pannonia, among others, as well as the wholesale changes made by Diocletian. The dispersal of military power in order to prevent coups d'état seems to have been the driving force, not that it was particularly successful. Changes were perhaps inevitable during the course of time, particularly when territory was first being occupied. By and large, the Romans left the internal organisation of a province much as they found it. This will be considered later; here it will be sufficient to note that the retention of a pre-conquest role title does not necessarily mean that its activities were unchanged.

Any fundamental changes were likely to be made clear to a governor as he prepared to take up his appointment. Before departure he would receive his terms of reference, known as *mandata*. They were probably in written form, although there could have been a verbal briefing. They described what must be done, might be done and what could not be done, together with the resources available to him for the attainment of his objectives. They could also imply the criteria by which his performance could be evaluated. We assume their content by the governor's subsequent actions, and we infer their prescribed and discretionary contents. They were essentially private instructions, not being officially published but setting out guiding principles and changes possible, together with any specific instructions particular to the situation in the province to which the governor was being sent. Pliny's correspondence, as we shall see, gives some indication of the latter.

The correspondence between Pliny the Younger and Emperor Trajan also suggests either that the discretionary element was relatively small, or that Pliny played on the side of caution. As we shall see, some of the matters on which he sought advice were minor. In some cases he was seeking retrospective approval for actions he had already taken. Julius Caesar gives a good example of a role description and *mandatum*. Prior to sailing for Britain he issued orders to his principal subordinate, Labienus, illustrating these aspects. First of all, Labienus was told he was to remain on the mainland where, second, he was allocated the command of three legions and two thousand cavalry. Third, with these resources he was required to guard the ports; fourth, he must ensure the corn supply and, fifth, keep himself informed about events in Gaul. Clearly these tasks were prescriptive. The discretionary element followed. He was 'to make plans as occasion and circumstance should require'. In other words, Labienus was authorised in other matters to use not only his own judgement but to act as he thought fit, without reference to his superior officer, Caesar (*Gallic War* 5.9).

Role relationships in an authority-based organisation are often expressed hierarchically, of which the army is a good example. The Emperor is commander-in-chief; the provincial governor is his subordinate as the general officer commanding the army in his province. In turn the legates of the legions are his subordinates, together with the commanders of the auxiliary units. Each of these has its own hierarchy of ranks within each unit. This is a relatively simple structure of role relationships, often represented vertically in a diagram. They can become more complicated when the relationship may be expressed horizontally. This is a collateral relationship. Here roles interact, but neither party has authority over the other. One person has to persuade another to provide him with a service;

only at a higher level is there someone who has authority over the affected roles. The relation between a governor and a procurator is a case in point. Both had their own executive systems, which were independent of each other. If there were a dispute it could only be resolved at the level of the Emperor, who exercised authority over all the disputants. The procurator had duties for which the governor had no responsibility, but he had another which impinged upon the governor, since he was paymaster of the army. Naturally, this was of concern to the governor. The viability of the army could depend on a satisfactory working relationship between the two officials. The action of Classicianus, the procurator in Britain, is an illustration of how this system worked. After the rising led by Boudicca he became alarmed by the continuing punitive policy of Suetonius Paulinus, because he considered it affected his own work. Economic recovery was being retarded. Reconciliation should be the first step to pacification, in which the fortunes of the province, to say nothing of the *fama* (reputation) of the Emperor, would depend. He made his views known at Rome, where his appreciation of the situation was accepted.

Augustus might declare himself to be no more than Princeps, First Citizen, but this modesty could not disguise his absolute power as the supreme authority in the state as head of state, chief executive, chief priest, and commander-in-chief of the army. The extant position was radically different from the formal; few could assume it to be otherwise. Writers like Tacitus might dream of 'the good old days', but even he recognised the properties of the situation. Augustus won power by the might of the sword: legitimacy came later, with the longevity of his rule, assisted by his style. The imperial regime was here to stay.

Nonetheless, the regime rested on the shoulders of the army. Having raised a victorious army, Augustus kept it onside throughout his life. He was able to nominate his most successful general, Tiberius, as successor, who not surprisingly had the support of the army. Gaius, who succeeded him without difficulty, had been as a child something of a favourite of the military, who named him Caligula ('Little Boots') after the miniature equipment they provided for him. His increasingly bizarre actions gradually revealed his unbalanced character. As a result he lost the confidence of senior officers in Rome, who assassinated him at the lunch break during a public event. No thought seems to have been given to a successor. It is said that a soldier found a hitherto little-known member of the imperial family – behind a curtain, it was thought – who was proclaimed Emperor as Claudius. As a thoroughly civilian Emperor who had been raised to the purple by a military clique stationed in Rome, he needed to secure the support of the units dispersed throughout the provinces by a demonstration of military capacity. The invasion of Britain seems to have been the result, made more plausible, probably, by conditions in the island. Aulus Plautius commanded the expeditionary force but he halted before Colchester, apparently the first objective of the campaign, so as to enable Claudius to command in person the final victorious engagement. The civilian had demonstrated his military capacity: the army was satisfied. Most of his successors either had or acquired *gloire militaire* sufficient to retain the loyalty of the army. If they did not, they fell. Nero's fall began when the army in Germany refused to take the *sacramentum*, the oath of loyalty, to him in January 69 CE. Thereafter different provincial forces promoted their own candidates, until Vespasian won supreme power. As Tacitus rightly wrote, the events of the year of the four Emperors demonstrated a new truth: Emperors could be made outside Rome by army units. He might, with justice, have added that it was not the provincials who made the political weather, but the armies stationed among them.

In the third century it got far worse as contenders – too numerous to mention here – vied for military support with bribes and extravagant promises. Either the army imposed its own candidate or the man proposed by others was acceptable to it. The rest of society had no option but to accept this politico-military reality; no alternative organisation seemed to possess the power to overthrow it. Remarkably, provincial life and governance seem to have remained relatively unaffected by these upheavals. The principle of subsidiarity paid off, as the officials of the civitates and cities continued largely unmolested in their roles. Furthermore, high officials of the provincial administration might remain in post unless there had been an unacceptable level of support for a defeated candidate. The central 'powers that be' in Rome were accepted with a degree of political realism: de facto power was more important than de jure authority. However, if an ambitious governor broke away from Rome, as did

Carausius in Britain, and if he won significant support from his officials, then, when his petty empire fell, his officials might fall with him, to be replaced by men on whose loyalty the successful Emperor could depend. Whether there was a purge of local minor government officials is more doubtful.

The stresses on the Empire in the west during the fifth century may have occasioned a quite different process. Confronted by invasions, provincial administration could begin to break down as officials were not replaced or paid. Some might be drafted into the service of successful invaders; others would have to fend for themselves. Provincial administration would fade away as personnel abandoned their roles. The process of decline could vary: it took longer in Britain than in Gaul, where it seems to have been accomplished within one generation. In Italy there were parallel administrations, at least for a time. In some ways the Church continued to manage aspects of local government, since it had its own well-organised structure ranging from local communities through provincial areas, and up to central government level. This, however, is beyond our immediate concern.

Finally, we should remember that organisations are not tangible. 'Most of the important aspects of an organisation … cannot be seen; we can read about them … try to understand what is going on in them, but we cannot "see" them … The process of examining an organisation is largely verbal rather than visual.' On this basis we can proceed, considering that the description of roles and role relationships, as well as the definition of such concepts as authority and power, may bring some grasp, with all its approximations and awareness of what may now be hidden from us, of Roman provincial administration, which not only lasted long but which is not without influence today.

CHAPTER 1

BOUNDARIES OF EMPIRE

Over a relatively short period the Republic and Empire acquired a large *imperium* whose centre was Rome and its outliers, situated largely round, or relatively near, the Mediterranean, acquired either by conquest or alliance, which led to absorption.

The Jews were a good example. Under the Maccabees they had fought with a good deal of success against the Seleucids, who dominated Asia Minor, Syria and Palestine, and had achieved a de facto freedom. The Seleucids, however, were always likely to attempt to recover lost domains on the one hand; on the other, the Ptolemies of Egypt were generally anxious to push their frontier through what is now the Gaza Strip into Palestine itself. The guerrilla leader Judas Maccabeus saw in the Romans a counterweight to these threats. The writer of the First Book of Maccabees is quite clear about the political significance of the treaty that was negotiated: 'Judas had heard of the reputation of the Romans, their military strength and their benevolence towards all who made common cause with them; they wanted to establish friendly relations with anyone who approached them, because of their military strength.' The writer goes on to say that the Jews knew of Roman conquests in Gaul, together with their exploitation of the mineral wealth of Spain, as well as their stunning successes in Asia Minor, adding, 'Where their friends and those who relied on them were concerned they had always stood by their friendship.' An embassy was sent to Rome specifically to lift the yoke of the Seleucids from their shoulders. The author then copied out the resolution of the Roman Senate, declaring it to have been engraved on bronze tablets with the words, 'Good fortune attend the Romans and the Jewish nation by sea and land for ever; may sword or enemy be far from them.' In brief, each side agreed to come to the aid of the other should either be attacked. To make the position clear, the text included a letter to be sent to Demetrius, the Seleucid king, threatening war against him if the Jews complained about his conduct (1 Maccabees 8).

Unfortunately, we are not always so well informed about the details of other alliances negotiated by the Romans. There is nothing comparable from Britain. The historians of the Republic might not have regarded any single alliance of much significance. The treaty, however, is of some importance as it does not come from the Roman side; it gives an insight into the way in which Roman influence could enhance its *imperium,* for Rome did not lose interest in those who entered into its orbit – they became absorbed. But there was a degree of reciprocity. The Jews did not forget Rome: Pompey was asked to arbitrate in a dispute about the High Priesthood; Julius Caesar negotiated a relationship favourable to them; Augustus accepted Herod's declaration of loyalty, making him 'A Friend of the Roman People' as a client king. Only after Herod's death did the clouds gather, leading to the campaigns of Vespasian, Titus and Hadrian which destroyed a Jewish polity for centuries to come.

At its greatest extent, the Roman Empire spanned much of Europe, North Africa and the Near East. In the west its frontier lay on the Atlantic seaboard and the Solway Firth; in the east towards the Tigris-Euphrates; to the north-east along the Rhine and in Central Europe along the Danube; in the south to the onset of the Sahara; in all some 4,000 kilometres west to east and 2,000 north to south. For a time it also embraced an area north of the Danube, occupying what is now Romania: the very name suggests the past.

However, the modern frontier is not the same as it was in Roman times. Today states think in terms of a sharply defined boundary, very often marked by a fence of some kind, with controlled entrances and exits. Sometimes geography can make this difficult, and frontier areas can be hard to police and control. Britain's frontier (limes) had both depth and defences: the line of Hadrian's Wall seems clear enough, but it had outlying forts to the north and south. Such a frontier could

The boundaries of the Empire set in stone; this reconstruction of the Roman fort of Arbeia at the eastern end of Hadrian's Wall shows the determination of Hadrian to exercise control over his northern frontier.

be considered militarily as defence in depth, with control points located at various points along the wall. Mountainous and desert areas might be controlled, not so much by a forward presence as by the management of communications on the routes along which people travelled, camped or traded.

The frontier between provinces cannot always be sharply defined, though the general area can be discerned, often from inscriptions. The concept of authority might be more important, since the Latin word *provincia* described the sphere of responsibility for a magistrate rather than a geographical zone. Its extension to territory followed. Further, a frontier may not have been sharply defined during the early stages of occupation.

Frontiers defining the boundary between the territories of tribes cannot be easily defined, though the general area may be indicated by remains. Roads could be a convenient boundary line when marked by an explanatory inscription erected by a local authority. For example, there is this milestone from Kenchester. When expanded it reads:

IMPERATORI CAESARI MARCO AURELIO NUMERIANO REPUBLICA
CIVITATIS DOBUNNOROUM.

For the Emperor Caesar Marcus Aurelius Numerianus, the civitas of the
Dobunni (set this up).

RIB 2250

Their capital was Cirencester. Their territory was adjacent to that of
the Silures of south-east Wales. The wording on the milestone could
be interpreted as putting down a boundary marker, rather than being
merely a declaration of loyalty.

Rivers could be a clear boundary line. However, like some roads, they
may be not merely points of closure but also lines of communication.
Traffic passes along them, and not merely over them, through customs
and security posts. The Rhine-Danube river systems should be
regarded in this way: Roman and barbarian met along them and not
just on either side of them. Social and commercial intercourse along
these channels could have a powerful cultural effect. Furthermore,
the lifestyle of farmers on either side of the limes might not often
be very different. The Goths, who were admitted into the Empire
in the fourth century, had been dealing with residents within the
Roman Empire across and along the limes for centuries before that
crossing. Romanisation may have been a policy of design, as Tacitus
suggests in *The Agricola* (18–21), and as the bronze tablets from York
seem to confirm (RIB 662, 663), but the informal contacts practised
over centuries could be more important than a specific education
programme. Nor should we assume the acculturation to be merely one
way, from Roman to non-Roman. Interaction was always possible.

The Empire was no ephemeral polity, but long-lasting. The time
span in the west was over 400 years; in the east it was more than
fourteen centuries. In this present work, however, we shall not
venture into the administration of the later Byzantine *imperium.* Our
curtain will come down as the Empire in the west collapses.

By the time Augustus had become Princeps, the Republic had
turned into a de facto monarchy embracing the Mediterranean
coasts, together with much of their hinterlands. Over the succeeding
centuries there were only a few additions, of which Britain was one.
Finally, Hadrian drew a line under further expansion; a decision, by
and large, observed by his successors.

There were numerous provinces. The Iberian Peninsula was divided into three: Lusitania in the south and west, Baetica in the south, and Tarraconensis, which embraced much of the midland, north and east as far as the Pyrenees. Over that mountain range lay Gaul, stretching eastwards as far as the Rhine and the Alps, with the Bay of Biscay and the English Channel forming the western and northern coastlines. The province of Narbonensis was in the south, Aquitania stood between the north-west of the Pyrenees and the Loire, Belgica occupied the land beyond the Seine as far as the Rhine, and Lugdunensis occupied the centre. Over the Rhine were Germania Inferior and Germania Superior, with Raetia to the east. Along the Danube and to its south were Noricum and Pannonia Inferior and Pannonia Superior. On the north side was Dacia, which had a relatively short life. Britain, having been invaded twice by Julius Caesar, was finally conquered in 43 CE and the following decades. It was divided into Britannia Prima and Britannia Secunda by Septimius Severus, and, like many other provinces, was heavily reorganised by Diocletian and his successors. Well to the south and somewhat to the east were Dalmatia and Macedonia, with Moesia Superior and Moesia Inferior nearby, and Thrace and Achaia further to the south. Across the Hellespont were the provinces of Asia Minor: Bithynia, Cappadocia and Galatia, Lycia, Pamphylia and Cilicia, with Cyprus off the coasts. Along the coast of the eastern Mediterranean were Syria and Palestine, with Arabia Patraea and Arabia itself. On the north-east coast of Africa was Egypt, lying along the banks of the Nile. The island province of Crete was to the north, Cyrenaica and Libya to the west, along with Numidia. In the north-west of Africa were Mauretania Tingitana and Mauretania Caesariensis. Finally, there was Italy, managed through the administration of eleven districts, but these will not be considered in the present study of provincial administration. The homeland was different.

Between west and east there were long-standing differences. In the former the tribe was the basic social and political unit, while in the latter the city-state had been characteristic. There were, however, some tribal units in the south-east, and Egypt, a kingdom of long standing, had its own distinctive organisation. As we shall see, Rome superimposed its own overarching structure, leaving the lower ranks of the hierarchy it inherited in some ways untouched, even though the terminology might be changed.

Not surprisingly, within the Empire was contained a variety of cultures accompanied by a plethora of languages. Under the Empire, however, the official government language of the west was Latin, with Greek serving the same purpose in the east. The east coast of the Adriatic was the approximate linguistic frontier. Translators were therefore necessary for the transaction of public business: in some areas it was sufficient to be bilingual, in others trilingual, in order to cope with local tongues. On the non-Roman side local leaders and entrepreneurs would find workaday Latin or koine Greek an advantage, while also needing their own translators to deal more precisely with Roman officers who in some cases would have either Latin or Greek as their second language. Linguistic Romanisation must have been necessary for the conduct of government within the provinces; without it communication would have been very difficult. Roman styles of dress, 'warm baths and elegant banquets' (*Agricola* 21) could come later, and even then they affected an urban elite far more than farming communities.

Edward Gibbon concluded his own tour of the provinces by observing how many fresh independent kingdoms arose out of the provinces of the Roman Empire, especially in the west. He wrote that it was easy for the inhabitants of the Empire to forget the 'outlying countries which had been left to the enjoyment of a barbarous independence, believing that the Roman *imperium* was coterminous with the globe of the Earth' (*Decline and Fall*, ed. J. B. Bury, vol. 1, p. 27). The inhabitants of the fifth-century Roman Empire were not to know what phoenixes would arise from the ashes of their misfortunes, nor that Caesar would become Kaiser in Germany, Shah in Iran, Czar in Russia; or that *Imperator* would become Emperor, nor indeed that the terms Legate and Procurator would remain in common use to this day. They could not foresee the architecture of the Congress building in Washington DC, still housing a Senate. Above all, they would not know that their law would continue to influence many legal systems even to this day, or that their language would be a fount for the Romance tongues spoken still in the present. As we turn to a study of provincial administration, we may glimpse how the transition was made.

CHAPTER 2

ROMANITAS

People, as well as their government, live in a culture, and sometimes more than one. They are partly inherited and partly refashioned in their own day and generation. There are complex movements whereby each affects the others. An overwhelming military victory, like Actium, may initiate major changes, but they may take a long time to be generally effective. A province may be conquered with relative ease, but its adoption of a Roman way of life, which we may call Romanisation, may take generations. External practice in adoption of certain styles of behaviour may be achieved quickly by official action, but to be self-sustaining they need to be under-girded by interior attitudes. In this way there can be successful acculturation. Agricola considered the Britons 'should become accustomed to peace and quiet by the provision of amenities' (*Agricola* 21). He encouraged individuals as well as communities to build temples, market places and town houses, as well as both to live and dress in the Roman style. Such were the visible signs. The adoption of Roman values required an education programme. The governor reached out to the coming generation of community leaders, having them educated in 'the liberal arts', for which there was an established curriculum. Agricola was pursuing a policy, begun by Augustus, aimed at creating a provincial culture which would bind the peoples together in loyalty to the Empire. This ideological endeavour could, over time, win hearts and minds and be more effective than mere military rule and physical occupation.

Augustus, though he may have come to power through bloodshed, realised a war-torn Republic needed peace and security. He stood forth as the bringer of peace: hence the significance of closing the Temple of Janus. He also strove to rehabilitate traditional values: hence his relatively unostentatious life style and modesty of dress. He may have appeared dressed as a general on his statues, but in life ordinarily 'he wore common clothes ... his togas were neither close nor full, his purple stripe neither narrow nor broad' and no insignia was carried save that of a consul. Suetonius also noted the modesty of his villas, while his domestic furnishings were simple. The Domus Augusti was no more than the residence of a nobleman; it was certainly not the palace of an absolute monarch (*Divus Augustus* 73).

It is by no means clear that others emulated him, seeming to prefer 'conspicuous consumption' instead. Personal example was not enough; a cultural programme was also necessary for both the capital and the provinces. The liberal arts were pressed into service to demonstrate Roman *virtus*, interpreted as everything excellent in both the physical and moral nature of humanity. Courage, loyalty, valour, bravery, respect for tradition were values to ensure the well-being of the state. By these, together with the appropriate rituals, the favour of the gods would be secured for eternity. The *Aeneid* of Virgil set this off to perfection. The destiny of Rome was marked out from the ruins of Troy and brought to Italy through the *virtus* of Aeneas (this superb epic brought the *Iliad* and *Odyssey* into a Roman perspective for those who could read Greek). It showed that there was a shape and purpose to history: Rome was fulfilling her destiny and Augustus was the agent. On this foundation there would be peace. Christian apologists would later sanctify this: the peace of Augustus made conditions right for the appearance of God's dedicated servant from Nazareth. Augustus had made possible universal peace. The message of salvation answered the policy of Augustus: 'Peace on Earth towards people of good will.'

The works of Cicero, Terence and Sallust filled out the curriculum but, over time, it might be supplemented. The *Eclogues* of Virgil also played their part in evoking the importance of farming and good estate management. Historians, too, such as Livy, also told a positive story. Readers were taken through events, leading them to appreciate the troubles experienced by previous generations, from which they had been delivered by the Bringer of Peace, Order and Quiet – virtues resting on the firm foundation of the old values now exemplified in the person of the Princeps and enhanced by the policies he pursued.

The two bronze plates from York set up, in Greek, by a *grammaticus* about 82 CE in the commander's headquarters in York hint at both the values and the policy. The text of Virgil found at Vindolanda in the household of a senior officer may be no more than the remains of a child's textbook; nonetheless, it indicates something of Roman culture in the officer class stationed in a province of the Empire. It was unlikely to be reading matter in the barrack blocks and even less so in the dwellings of the civil settlement, but over decades, even centuries, by various routes a sense of *Romanitas* seems to have suffused the provinces, where lifestyle, values and practices were more important than mastery of the literary classics. A note of caution should be sounded, however; rural peasant communities were likely to be relatively untouched. Large villas occupied by leaders who commuted between them and their town houses were no doubt the bearers of Roman culture in both town and countryside. Inevitably, provinces would also vary in the degree of Romanisation: a good deal depended upon the vitality of the pre-Roman culture of the province. Achaia was different from Antioch, and both differed from Londinium. Acculturation was a two-way process, with varying balances in the provinces, but it was probably promoted more by day-to-day contacts than any official programme.

Roman law also played a significant role in provincial administration. First of all, there was its effect upon the administrators in so far as they were citizens, but second, for its impact upon local laws. These two strands acted as a force to bind people together. During the Republic a good legal system had emerged; under the Empire it was developed, not abrogated. Over time laws had become somewhat systemised, through three stages:

1) The pre-classical period, prior to the Principate;

2) The classical period of the Principate. During this period, legal thought was much advanced by great jurists like Gaius, Papinian, Ulpian and Paulus. Under Augustus the right of replying to questions of law (*jus respondendi*) was granted to distinguished jurists. As

the *imperium* developed, the Emperor came to possess unrestricted legislative powers, classified as *constitutiones*, under five heads:

i *Edicta*: proclamations issued in his capacity as chief magistrate;

ii *Mandata*: prescriptive instructions to subordinates like provincial governors;

iii *Decreta*: judicial decisions, especially those given on appeal;

iv *Rescripta*: written answers to those who had consulted the Emperor on a point of law. Replies by inferior magistrates were known as *epistolae*. The replies to questions submitted by private citizens were described as *subscriptiones*;

v *Orationes*: the submission of a bill to the Senate (a feature of the earlier Empire);

3) The post-classical period of the third century during which, as absolutism increased, so did legislation by imperial decree grow.

The whole would be codified later, during the rule of Justinian. Of interest to us are the *mandata* and *rescripta*, to which reference will be made when the role of the governor is studied.

The praetor urbanus was a magistrate of the Republic who was responsible for the administration of justice. A praetor peregrinus was appointed to deal with cases involving foreigners. Gaius, in his *Institutes*, points out that very 'extensive law is contained in the edicts of the two praetors, the urban and the peregrine, whose jurisdiction is possessed in the provinces by the provincial governors', indicating an important aspect of the governor's role, connecting it with the legal system as a whole, and explaining their formal title, legatus augusti pro praetore, i.e. for the praetor and with praetorian authority. He adds that the edicts of the curule aediles also have extensive legal powers, 'whose jurisdiction is possessed in the provinces of the Roman people by quaestors; no quaestors are sent to the provinces of Caesar' (1.6). The general principles by which the praetor intended to be guided during his period in office were set out in the *Edictum Perpetuum*, which did not mean that it lasted forever, but was operative continuously during that time. Under Hadrian the edicts of the praetors were consolidated.

Roman law comprised both public and private law, and all citizens were subject to them. However, most of the population were not citizens until later; they were members of communities, with their own laws and customs which existed before they were brought within the Roman orbit. Of these, perhaps the most accessible to us is the Jewish Torah. A governor and his administration as a whole were inevitably faced with the correlation between Roman and local law. The praetor peregrinus, as the official concerned with foreigners, would need to take account of this situation. On the one hand these people were foreigners, but on the other, since they were now subject to Roman rule, they were, in a sense, foreigners no longer. Some process of assessment would be needed of these local laws, to decide how far they were compatible with at least the principles of Roman law. Unacceptable elements would have to be removed, and any deficiencies made up. The rules of some religions might well be excised, with punishments promulgated for following them. Once this process had been completed, a revised corpus could be endorsed for use in the appropriate local government units. The treatment of Jesus and James seem to demonstrate this (Mark 15; Acts 12.2 ff.). Of particular interest for provincial administration in this process were the concepts of *jus naturale* and *jus gentium. Jus* meant both the rules of law and the rights conferred on a person by those rules in a particular situation. Gaius defined *jus naturale* as 'what nature has taught all living things', implying there were rules of universal application derived from the common nature of all peoples. The concept was not unconnected with the *logos* propounded by Stoicism, a philosophy popular with many in Roman public life. A spark of the divine *logos* lived in each person, binding them together in a common humanity. As Marcus Aurelius put it, we must remember that even the one who opposes us is 'a fellow creature, similarly endowed with reason and a share of the divine'. The rules of the *jus naturale* should be observed by all humanity. It was the ideal to which all laws should be directed. The *jus gentium* was the law of other nations found to be in use among civilised peoples, but it was also that part of Roman law applicable to the relationship between Roman citizens and foreigners living within the jurisdiction of their law. Originally used for legal matters in commerce, it came to have a general application and superseded the *jus civile,* which was 'the law each people has settled for itself and is peculiar to the State itself' as the *Institutes* define it. The *jus gentium,* in a general way, allowed Roman administrators not to destroy but, up to a certain level, endorse the legal systems of the tribes and states they absorbed.

The overall jurisdiction of a governor was not impugned by this kind of local provision. He moved round his province with some regularity, holding a *conventus*, known to us as an assize, where he dispensed justice in cases brought before him either by the local authorities, or perhaps in some cases by the centurion or legate of a region. The provincial administration always retained a reserve and overriding authority. We need not assume that it was only at the assizes when justice was done. A governor may have had a law court sitting permanently at his provincial capital. Nor should we assume a governor would hear all cases himself. We know of the appointment of *legati iuridici,* as in Britain (CIL 2864). A quaestor at the governor's headquarters or some other nominated person might act with delegated authority from the governor. This is particularly true of the tribes who inhabited the western world. The courts of *civitates* (local authorities) were permitted to administer justice, civil and criminal, according to their own laws, customs and practices. The Jews were able to appoint their own judges for both civil and criminal cases. The criteria were that a man should be free, an adult and Jewish. There seemed to be no need to get approval or clearance from the provincial administration. Serious cases, however, and in particular capital offences, would generally come before a governor or quaestor on circuit. The details of such laws are often hidden from us, since many tribes possessed an oral rather than a written tradition, with one notable exception. The Jewish scriptures preserve the laws of their nation. The Christian New Testament shows something of the extent to which the laws of this people were, within certain limits, accepted. As a Roman citizen, Paul could override them in his hour of need, and a disgruntled person could always try to appeal to a governor over the head of his local judges; whether he would be successful was another matter.

There was thus a two-tier system operating throughout the Empire, united at the point of final appeal. This combination of Roman and local laws helped to weld the Empire together by creating a sense of identity – of a *Romanitas* whose strength would be displayed later in the stresses induced by the invasions of peoples with a radically different life style. But even before then they helped to unite the disparate, but essential, elements of the mixed society which made up the Empire, to give, along with the empowerment of local authorities, common ground on which they and Roman provincials could stand, producing a sense of common identity and not only ensuring loyalty to Roman *imperium* but also transmitting a rich legacy to the new emerging states. There was, however, a dark side, where Rome and all its works were hated for their persecuting brutality. The later chapters of the Book of Revelation in the Christian New Testament bear witness to that. For the writer Rome was Babylon, the Scarlet Woman and the Great Prostitute (Revelation 17, 18). The Christianity of the second century did not appear sympathetic to *Romanitas*; but other religions were able to make their contribution. They could and did promote a sense of unity. Religion was socially useful, especially in ensuring the support of the gods for the well-being of the Empire.

Religion thus had its bonding uses. The Latin word *religio* refers to that which is divine, wholly other than the human: something inscrutable but impinging on human life, and thus requiring a response through rites and ceremonies. The Graeco-Roman world was not monotheistic, but it was religious. Almost everything in the world possessed its own guardian spirit, and in that sense Earth was indeed 'crammed with heaven'. Philosophers might appear sceptical of much of all this, but on the whole they played their part in the public rituals. Both Cicero and the Younger Pliny observed them. We would be wrong to think that the old religions had faded during Empire; epigraphy points to the contrary. Diverse cults clearly sat alongside each other, helping to bind society. Romans who adhered to their traditional gods nonetheless assimilated other deities by a process of equivalence. Greek Zeus became Jupiter, Artemis was Diana, and Sulis of Bath became identified with Minerva. Druids may have been beyond the pale: Julius Caesar was highly critical of them, regarding them as a highly organised cult opposed to Rome. Tacitus lends some credence to the latter in his references to the conquest of Anglesey or Mona (*Annals* 14.30; *Agricola* 18). In the *Annals*, the preliminaries to battle are accompanied by a description of rampaging women who encouraged the defenders and strove to terrorise the attackers. Druidism may be more associated with magical practices than a description of a specific cult. It is hard to see any druidical significance in the funerary and dedicatory inscriptions set up in

Britain. After Mona was subdued, it seems to disappear from the records: what went on in secret can only be surmised.

There was some suspicion of oriental mystery religions, partly because of their secrecy but also because they could not be associated easily with the received cults; nor did they seem to promote the traditional purpose of religion in presenting a public communal face to the gods. Nonetheless the cults made significant progress, especially in the eastern provinces. Mithraism became popular in the army; at one time, it might have become the Empire's state religion. The Jews were the exception, being specifically tolerated. Their leaders' contention that their religion forbade sacrifice to a human was accepted, but they added that they were willing to sacrifice daily on behalf of the Emperor. Their revolts brought that arrangement to an end.

The cult of Roma was placed over all the individual cults, focusing upon both the city and the Emperor. A pinch of incense or a libation on an altar, or before a statue, were the satisfactory hallmarks of loyalty: they were the outward and visible sign of commitment to the Roman *imperium*. Provincial councils, government officers, as well as the army, all took the *sacramentum*. The refusal of Christians to observe this protocol when required to do so led to their punishment. They were regarded as atheists for their refusal to participate in civic rites. Loyal obedience, in word and good behaviour, as urged by New Testament writers, was insufficient (I Peter 2.13–15, and Romans 13); there must be an outward act to symbolise the inward commitment. The imperial cult promoted the deification of Emperors. Originally a Greek practice (Alexander had been deified), it was taken up in the Empire, but Augustus never accepted divine honours, though as the adopted son of Julius Caesar, who had himself been deified, he could easily have done, since he was by descent a son of god. Others succumbed, but usually after death, by resolution of the succeeding government.

The catastrophes of the third and fourth centuries caused much heart-searching among the Roman elite. Had the gods of old deserted the Empire? Were they offended by imperfect worship or by the admission of erroneous cults? These were the sort of questions that led to the persecution of Christians, but they were also an indication of the extent to which religion with its appropriate practices was regarded as a significant means of holding the Empire together. A change of god might renew the Empire. The importance of Constantine here is the choice he made, to make Christianity the bedrock of the Empire. The Christian god had blessed him; a further benediction might come if the Empire turned the same way. This was the birth of Christendom: to be Roman was to be Christian; to be Christian was to be Roman. That would be both a strength in the days of Empire, but a potential weakness in dealing with conquering barbarian non-Christian settlers, who might not be worthy of the Gospel since they lacked *Romanitas*.

Paradoxically, the imperial adoption of Christianity, together with its consequent expansion to a dominant position, divided the Empire in a way that the old polytheism did not. The latter had a large element of live and let live: it was more a matter of ritual than doctrine. By the fourth century, Christianity had acquired a strong dogmatic element with a variety of doctrines, the most important of which centred on the person of Jesus of Nazareth. The government regarded religious unity to be necessary for the wellbeing of the Empire: it not only adopted its own doctrinal position, but sought to enforce its opinion. Stringent measures were taken from time to time against those who persisted in maintaining a different viewpoint. Thus division was caused, made worse by imperial doctrines changing periodically as the views of the government varied with the outlook of succeeding Emperors. The Empire might become Christian, but what would constitute orthodoxy? The rulers in church and state argued long and hard. A council might proclaim a doctrine, but it often served to exacerbate dissent rather than solve the problem.

Roman Britain was not much affected by these controversies. Water Newton may have produced the earliest Eucharistic vessels known in the Empire; the faith may have been steadily practised; but no theological treatises have come down to us. During the fifth century the papacy thought the British were afflicted with the Pelagian heresy. This impression may have been given by the learned British monk, Pelagius, whose views were condemned in Rome. If, indeed, the congregations of Britain did follow him, this could demonstrate a degree of theological sophistication for which there is little evidence. However, given conditions in the province where the population, Christian or not, were struggling to survive as pagan invaders pushed their way into the island, a 'practical' Pelagianism might have an appeal. Deprived of resources by the central government and exhorted to deal with the situation themselves, Pelagius' teaching that people could take the first steps to salvation themselves, as opposed to waiting for prior divine initiatives, might strengthen the British will. There was no virtue in waiting for other sources of aid: the government had made clear none would be forthcoming. In their situation, Augustine's prayer, 'Grant what thou commandest and command what thou wilt,' might seem to exhort passivity upon a people struggling to preserve their independent way of life.

The Latin language was the medium through which many of these elements not only found expression, but were bound together. It was the linguistic bond of Empire, not so much in the polished style of a metropolitan elite, but in the workaday speech of workshop, tavern, market place, law court and administration. For many indigenous people in the provinces, it would always be their second language. Of this Latin we have relatively little knowledge. The Vindolanda writing tablets have been almost as much a revelation as the discovery of koine Greek was in the nineteenth century. The grammar is simpler and the vocabulary contains words rarely, if ever, found in modern dictionaries.

Too much, however, should not be claimed for Latin. Greek held its own as the lingua franca of the east, but again it was the language of the workaday world, not of Attica. In order to deal with this, the imperial secretariat had its own Greek department. Cultured Romans were often literate in the language; it helped hold Byzantium together for centuries. For some time Greek was the language of worship and literature in Christianity; to this day, fragments may be found in the Eucharist. Yet even in the east, Latin might obtrude. The inscription mentioning Pontius Pilate in the theatre at Caesarea Maritima (the capital of the province of Judaea) is in Latin. He ordered the charge on which Jesus was crucified to be exhibited not only in Hebrew, the ordinary language of the Jews, but also in both Greek and Latin (John 19.20). The first two might have been reasonably expected, but not perhaps the third. The practice may have been common for public notices.

We can see how successful, over time, with the acquisition of *Romanitas* all this was by studying the nature of societies emerging from the collapse of the Empire in the west. There is enough here to think in terms of transformation rather than obliteration. Leaders who fought against Rome came to admire it and all it stood for. The rule of Theodoric shows how successfully *Romanitas* was bequeathed to the new rulers. Roman provincial administration may have become deprived of supervision by the imperial government, but it could be harnessed into service by the new rulers, to whom officials became accountable. It would become the means through which government was carried on for the issue of decrees and the collection of taxes. As we shall see later on, the organisation of the Christian Church continued relatively unimpaired, to be able to preserve a good deal of *Romanitas* through leaders, scholarship and liturgy. By the fall of the Empire in the west it was already using the terms of Diocletian's reformed provincial administration.

CHAPTER 3

CENTRAL GOVERNMENT

The battle of Actium (2 September 31 BCE) brought twenty years of civil war in the Roman Republic to an end. Octavianus had won. Mark Antony committed suicide after his defeat. Cleopatra followed, after failing to win over the victor who also ensured the death of her son, Caesarion, by Julius Caesar. The Republic was his. Octavianus was possessed of overwhelming force, with a large army, funded by him, at his command; a Republic weary of strife lay at his feet, with potentially absolute power in his hands. The rule of one man might at least end decades of political and military conflict. The provincials might think this would be better than being exploited by greedy, harsh Republican magistrates. The doors of the Temple of Janus were closed (29 BCE): peace had been restored at last.

But had the Republic, indeed, been restored? Had old freedoms been discovered afresh? Formally it might seem to be the case; in practice it did not appear to be so, and though a few might have lamented the demise of the Republic, most seemed to accept that power rested with one man, now given the title of Augustus (which we might translate as 'Right Honourable and Very Reverend'), upon whom authority had been conferred. By degrees it became clear that Rome and its provinces were ruled by an absolute monarch, who preserved the magistracies of the Republic in his own person. He conducted a census (28 BCE), after which he reduced the Senate to some 800 members from about 1,000. Later, the number was taken down to 600. He increased the financial requirements for becoming a senator, and was allowed to create patrician families. He was declared Princeps Senatu. Augustus transferred authority over the state to the Senate and People of Rome, but received a number of provinces (e.g. Gaul, Syria and Spain), thus taking a proconsular role, while retaining his consulship. He became commander-in-chief of the army and so imperator. He also assumed the office of Pontifex Maximus, and as a result took charge of religious practices. Adopted by Julius Caesar, who had been declared *divus* – a god – Augustus himself became a son of god; in some sense a saviour. An oath of allegiance, the *sacramentum*, was demanded of the provinces, together with their officials. In particular, the army took an oath of loyalty to his person. All this, combined with his wealth and military resources, made the position clear: Rome was indeed an imperial autocracy. Formal statements, titles and outward forms may all be deceptive. Augustus may have been designated Princeps, First Citizen, but the imperium was controlled by one man, who ruled it from his household. His treasury, the Fiscus Caesari, overtook the Republican treasury, the Aerarium Populi Romani, in power and importance; most of the provincial revenues went into the former. His officials became the imperial officers. A salaried administrative service came into existence, whose remuneration often appeared in documents and upon inscriptions; for example LX, an official receiving 60,000 sesterces, C or HSC, 100,000, CC or HSCC, 200,000, and CCC or HSCCC, 300,000. The backbone of this bureaucracy was the equestrian order, to which freedmen and slaves could be added, and periodically his freedmen. The Senate lost its independence as an executive, though it remained a consultative body, but more importantly it served as a human resources pool from which high officials could be drawn.

Our concern here is not to describe the central government in detail, but to correlate it with the administration of the provinces. The effective governance of well over thirty of them required an adequate supply of men to fill not only gubernatorial posts, but also the staff required within the senior levels of the hierarchy. Since appointments were either time-bound or at imperial pleasure, there was a constant turnover of men in and out of appointments without unnecessary vacancies.

For the provincial administration there were five main sources of recruitment:

Men of senatorial rank, or on the way to achieving it
Equestrians
Imperial freedmen
Imperial slaves
Army personnel, to posts from sections 1 and 2 above

A career pattern developed for those of senatorial and equestrian rank to which we must pay attention later. The use of freedmen could often be resented, especially if they held major appointments. Tacitus makes a particular point about the staff used by Agricola: 'he made no use of freedmen or slaves for official business' (*Agricola* 19). Claudius was fortunate that when Narcissus, a freedman who was one of his principal ministers, appeared before the army in an attempt to overcome their reluctance to embark for the *terra incognita* of Britain, a fiasco was avoided when the troops perceived his presence humorously by calling 'O saturnalia', the winter solstice event when the social order was reversed. What discipline had not achieved, a sense of incongruity did: the troops went on board forthwith.

Entrance into the senatorial order was conferred by the Emperor. The subsequent career pattern was known as the cursus honorum: the sequence of honours, actually magistracies. It began with a pre-senatorial stage for young men aged about eighteen, of free birth, who possessed the requisite property qualification. There was an annual entry into what was known as the viginitivirate, i.e. The Twenty Men.

They were divided into four working sections:

A board of three: the tres viri monetales, mint masters, who were responsible for the production of copper coins for the Senate.

A group of ten: viri stilitibus, who were concerned with the making of judgements in civil disputes.

Four men acting as assistant to the aediles in maintaining the streets of Rome: the quatuorviri viarum curandarum.

Tres viri capitales, acting as assistants to the judiciary and responsible for capital punishment.

Augustus was the architect of what became the Roman Empire, together with the procedures of provincial administration largely described in this book.

The last group were the least prestigious; the monetales had the most. All patricians seem to have begun their careers on this board. It has been argued that the allocation of these postings indicated the pattern of their future careers. However, at eighteen these young men had nothing to show on their curriculum vitae. Moreover, their roles may have been more 'work experience' than executive management. There must have been a degree of dependence on the more permanent staff. In any case, the ability to create an impression is not the same thing as a demonstration of capacity; no doubt they could be fast-tracked, but competence would normally have to be demonstrated. The promise at eighteen had to be fulfilled by results in later life. Subordinates cannot easily cover personal inadequacies throughout all stages of a career.

The next step was service as a military tribune, tribunus laticlavus (tribune of the broad stripe), a posting that could last between one and three years.

At twenty-four men could enter the Senate as quaestor. There were twenty-four entrants each year: two or more were attached as aides to the Emperor, ten were assigned to the proconsuls. The remainder

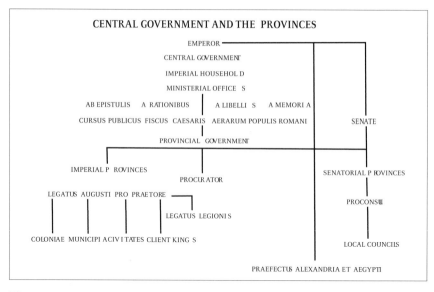

CENTRAL GOVERNMENT AND THE PROVINCES

EMPEROR

CENTRAL GOVERNMENT

IMPERIAL HOUSEHOLD

MINISTERIAL OFFICES

AB EPISTULIS   A RATIONIBUS   A LIBELLIS   A MEMORIA

CURSUS PUBLICUS FISCUS CAESARIS AERARUM POPULIS ROMANI   SENATE

PROVINCIAL GOVERNMENT

IMPERIAL PROVINCES   SENATORIAL PROVINCES

PROCURATOR

LEGATUS AUGUSTI PRO PRAETORE   PROCONSUL

LEGATUS LEGIONIS

COLONIAE MUNICIPI ACIVITATES CLIENT KINGS   LOCAL COUNCILS

PRAEFECTUS ALEXANDRIA ET AEGYPTI

Diagram 1

were stationed in Rome. A year's 'sabbatical' followed this, after which a man became either tribunus plebis (of the people) or an aedile. Patricians were excused this appointment. Another 'sabbatical' came after the completion of this role.

At twenty-nine came the praetorship, of which there were twelve (later more), the post being held for a year. In the course of time it became more of an honorary appointment. Then, at about the age of forty-two, came the consulship. There were two consules ordinarii, who were often stood down after holding the appointment for but a short time. They were replaced by consules suffecti, who might also stand down within the year. There might have been as many as twelve consuls within a calendar year; however, these temporary appointments helped to ensure a sufficient supply of men of both requisite rank and experience for provincial service. They had served not only in Rome but in at least one province, as well as in the army. They had also acquired administrative and judicial experience.

Twenty-four legionary legates (legatus legionis) were needed at any time, of whom at least five, rising to fourteen, would become a governor: legatus augusti pro praetore. Four iuridici were required, two for Tarraconensis, one each for Britain and Galatia-Cappadocia.

They served for two to three years. The appointments may have been occasional rather than sequential; it depended on local conditions. A man might be appointed curator civitates or curator Republicae, supervising the administration of a town or area. It was most unusual for a man to return more than once to a location or unit. Agricola's cursus was the exception, for he held several in Britain. Finally, there could be occasional ad hoc appointments made as a result of particular situations whose nature is largely closed to us. The point is that no administration can be effective unless it has the degree of flexibility necessary for the efficient transaction of business.

A governor not only had to communicate with the Emperor, he had to deal with senior ministers. Of these, two were important: a rationibus, who was the minister of finance, and ab epistulis, who managed the imperial chancery and through whom most communications would pass. Periodically some contact might be necessary with a libellis (where there were short-hand writers), who could give up-to-date information about codes and ciphers; he might turn to a memoria if he needed access to official files. For access to all these he would need authorised imperial permission for couriers to use the cursus publicus, which gave access to mansiones, accommodation and stabling, as well as relays of horses. The channel would also be needed by the procurators – men of equestrian rank – to whose career structure we now turn.

Equestrians were of free birth and possessed of at least 400,000 sesterces. They formed the backbone of the Roman middle class, if that term may be used in the ancient world, with all its breadth and ambiguity. Over time, equestrians came to play an ever-increasing role in the governance of the Empire. The provincial governor and his staff met them at various points, first of all as the ab epistulis, through whose office communications would normally pass. Next there would be financial affairs, especially those relating to the army stationed in the governor's province, handled by a rationibus. From time to time he might wish to draw on the services of a libellis and a memoria, particularly if his provincial files did not hold the relevant information. All these roles were occupied by equestrians. Office holders were graded according to the degree of authority conferred upon them, and this was reflected in their salary. The scale ranged from 60,000 sesterces, recorded as sexagenarius, which was

The inscription of a consul ordinarius in the Roman Colosseum. The two ordinary consuls took office on 1 January, and the year following was named after them for dating purposes. Resignation might follow after a short time; a replacement was known as a suffectus. The process ensured the supply of ex-consulars capable of taking up senior appointments reserved for that rank.

the starting point, through 100,000 – centarius, on to ducenarius at 200,000 and at a later period to 300,000 as a trecenarius. For all of these grades, there were abbreviations as described above.

Men came from a variety of backgrounds. Generally they had served in the army before they entered civilian appointments. At the pinnacle of the career structure stood four prefectures: three held in Rome in charge of the annona, the vigiles and the Praetorian Guard; but of most interest to us, in provincial administration, was the prefecture of Egypt. In the middle to higher rankings were the procurators, imperial finance agents, to whom a later chapter is devoted.

These two categories of office holders administered the provinces, which were of two kinds: imperial, described by Gaius as provinces of Caesar, while the others were known as the provinces of the Roman people, commonly described today as senatorial provinces. The imperial provinces were those in which there was a significant military presence, mainly where there was a frontier of Empire such as the two Germanies, the Pannonias, Syria, and Britain. Here the governors were commanders of the army alongside their role as the dispensers of justice, hence their description as legatus augusti, the officer of the Emperor, with praetorian powers, pro praetore. The senatorial provinces, with troops mainly devoted to the protection of the provincial staff, were managed by a pro-consul who acted, technically, on behalf of the consuls who chaired the Senate.

Overall, the system produced men with experience of both military and civilian roles, but an examination of senatorial careers shows that a career might be biased towards one side or the other. The early governors of Britain were military men. The cursus of Agricola and of Pliny illustrate the point.

Tacitus, whose own career was mainly civilian, makes no mention of the service of his father-in-law in the viginitivirate, but might be presumed as not worthy of notice. Born about 40 CE, Agricola became a military tribune in Britain (of senatorial rank) in 58 CE. In 63/64 he moved on to be a quaestor in the Province of Asia (a senatorial province) and then he became a tribune of the people, tribunus plebis, in 66 CE, to be followed by a praetorship in 68 CE. In 70 CE he was legatus legionis of Legio XX in Britain, moving on to be governor of Aquitania between 73 and 76 CE and then consul in 76 CE, after which he was appointed legatus augusti pro praetore in Britain. With that, his career closed. The military emphasis is clear: what is exceptional is that so many postings were to Britain.

We should hesitate to over-emphasise the degree of specialisation. It was inevitable that a province like Britain, or indeed any other when being conquered and then pacified, should be governed by a man who had significant military experience. The presence of a large garrison also demanded a governor who could be an effective general officer.

Conversely, a province in financial difficulty required a man with financial capacity: someone like Pliny. The younger Pliny was born about 61 CE. After studying law he became a tribune with a legion in Syria, about 81 CE. In about 90 CE he became a praetor, which was followed by two prefectures, first of the aerari militaris and second of the aerari Saturni, both of them treasury roles. He became consul about 100 CE, followed by an appointment as curator alvei Tiberis, supervising the maintenance of the river banks. Then he became a judicial adviser to Trajan's council, and his career closed with his appointment as legatus augusti in Bithynia-Pontus, specially charged to reform its chaotic finances. He may well have died in office, or soon after.

Communications with provincial officials and any with whom the Emperor wished to deal were despatched by the staff of the cursus publicus, which with its accommodation (known as mansiones) built at frequent intervals, and stabling for relays of horses, provided an effective system. The facility could be used only with the permission of the Emperor, which was not lightly given.

These were the principal officials and their departments with which provincial governors had to deal. Formally, the Senate supervised the administration of its provinces and appointed their officials; however, it was prudent to know that any given action or appointment had the approval, support, or at least the good will of the Emperor. To act contrary to his wishes was risky and relatively rare. That is the nature of a single absolute authority. There was no need to micro-manage

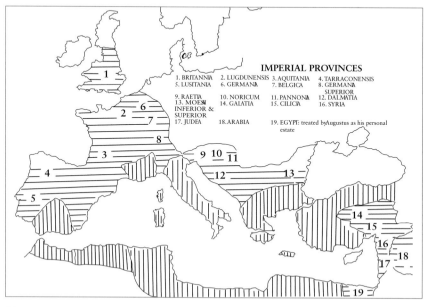

Diagram 2

This early third-century inscription from Caerwent shows how an official could move from a senatorial to an imperial province as well as from a military to an administrative command. For more details, see Appendix.

affairs: in such a regime, other organisations and people could be managed at a distance if the chief executive's wishes were known, along with the extent of the discretionary element contained in any role. The Emperor could always contract that authority to himself in any matter engaging his attention. There was, therefore, a reserve power of veto, or at least a fear of imperial displeasure and consequent loss of favour which acted as regulative power over a subordinate. The grammateus (chief executive) of Ephesus understood this when successfully quelling a riot. A high-level official investigation, he told the mob, was highly likely. They dispersed (Acts 19.40–41).

In some ways this apparatus appears modest, considering the extent of the Empire; however, there were other elements adding to the governance of the state. As we shall see later when considering local government, there was a high degree of subsidiarity within the imperial organisational structure. This pushed many aspects of civil administration down to local communities, for which they were held accountable. In addition, the Emperor had parallel lines of government. Finance, including not only imperial estates but provincial revenues, as well as army pay, came under the control of provincial procurators, who were imperial nominees reporting directly to the Emperor, and not to and through the provincial governor. This twin track of accountability could strengthen the position of the central government. It could be a case of 'divide and rule'.

Finally, the role of the army was important in the imperial provinces. Care had to be taken to ensure its loyalty, as well as that of the province as a whole. The former swore an oath annually; the council of the latter passed a resolution. The younger Pliny took care to ensure that Trajan knew he and his province had reaffirmed their loyalty to their Emperor, who replied thanking him for this message. If the Empire was an absolute monarchy, it was one resting in the last resort upon the military. Keep the soldiers happy, said Septimius Severus to his son, and forget the rest. Such was the *realpolitik* of empire.

In an imperial province, the governor's staff included a large number of military personnel who occupied administrative roles. Soldiers could be posted on secondment from their units to undertake specific duties in the headquarters building, or they might be sent out to undertake supervisory duties as occasion required, in any given area. The governor himself would have had military experience before taking up his appointment, whose job description included that of being general officer commanding of the units stationed in his province. The legates of the legions were accountable to him, and through them the commanders of auxiliary units within the area of their legionary districts.

In addition, soldiers might act as customs officials on the frontiers of a province, as on Hadrian's Wall. There does not seem to have been any official accommodation provided for civilian staff, either in the forts or in nearby civil settlements. Provincial officials might well have required something better than the housing and facilities available in nearly civil settlements. Some demobilised senior centurions were recruited into the provincial administration (retaining their rank), and no doubt if necessary, if still single, they might be accommodated in barracks. Had they married, a dwelling in a civil settlement might then be tolerable. It would be interesting to know the residential arrangements made.

The military might also assist in a variety of civilian tasks, from building projects to regional supervision. The army was far more than a fighting force: it was connected formally and informally with the government of provinces and of the Empire as a whole.

Finally, we should bear in mind that these government posts, centrally and provincially, were not filled at random but by means of the structured process. Men were drawn from distinct social classes. The Emperor drew upon senators or those of the senatorial class for the viginitivirate, curatores, praefecti urbi, legatus augusti and legatus legionis. For the praefectus vigilum, annonea, vehiculorum, praetorio, procurator and praefectus Alexandriae et Aegypti, he drew upon equestrians. For the roles of a rationibus and ab epistulis (to the irritation of traditionalists like Tacitus), imperial freedmen might often be employed: men who were often highly educated accomplished 'mandarins'. They worked within a structured hierarchy where salary reflected both responsibility and status.

The central government thus consisted of a variety of roles, possessed of defined tasks and constituted in a structure of role relationships in which there were different levels of accountability and authority, but at the head of which stood the Emperor as the supreme authority, to whom everyone was finally accountable. This was the executive system for the imperial administration, by which the provincial administration was shaped and through whose senior office holders it was accountable to the Emperor.

Reports from provincial governors could also be read to the Senate. Originally it was the council of the monarchs; under the Republic it remained as an advisory body to the magistrates. Augustus regarded its preservation as a necessary outward and visible sign of the supposed restoration of the Republic. Under the principate it ceased to have executive powers throughout the Empire; its status was retained, but not its overall executive functions. Its formal status did not cohere with its extant position. Few, if any, thought it did. Some executive functions remained, however: the government of Italy, together with a number of provinces, containing few or no troops. Nonetheless, senators were well advised to ensure their appointees were *persona grata* to the Emperor. Elections to the Senate also had to have regard to the will of the Emperor. This reduced the importance of elections to a minimum. Further, the Emperor, by means of *ad lectio*, could always introduce new members into the chamber. The debates which took place in the house were likely to be supportive rather than critical: strong dissent was dangerous. More significantly for provincial government, the senatorial class provided a pool from which administrators could be drawn for senior appointments.

CHAPTER 4

THE GOVERNOR IN OFFICE

Once nominated, the governor was free to appoint his personal staff. Others on the official provincial establishment would be awaiting him on his arrival in his province. They constituted a considerable hierarchy, ranging from a chief of staff through to adjutants, clerks, grooms and bodyguards. In imperial provinces, soldiers of varying ranks occupied many of the roles. We need not assume they constituted a service made up of permanent officials: there appears to have been a rotation of personnel from both legionary and auxiliary units, but no doubt the governor would be able to make senior appointments himself if he wished; otherwise the process could be handled by his chief of staff, or perhaps an adjutant.

This constituted the core of the internal administrative executive system for managing the government of the province. External communications were with the local government units, the procurator and his staff, and other governors, but above all with the central government, the Emperor and his ministers. If the letters published by the younger Pliny are any guide, a frequent exchange took place. There was little to indicate that a governor was left to his own devices. Allowance must be made for the nature of the publication. Trajan is always the respondent. There must, however, have been messages where the reverse was the case. It could have been imprudent to reveal them.

The correspondence started while Pliny was on his way to Bithynia:

I am sure, Sir, you will be interested to hear that I have rounded Cape Malea and arrived at Ephesus, with my complete staff. My intention now is to travel on to my province partly by boat and partly by carriage. The intense heat prevents my travelling entirely by road, and the Etesian winds make it impossible to go all the way by sea.

Trajan replies sympathetically:

My dear Pliny, you did well to send me news, for I am much interested to know what sort of journey you are having to your province. You are wise to adapt yourself to local conditions and travel either by boat or carriage.

Another letter follows, telling Trajan that Pliny's health was good but he found the heat still trying. A touch of fever had held him up at Pergamum; however, he was on his way, entering his province formally on 17 September – the Emperor's birthday. Pliny goes on to inform Trajan that he has begun work already by examining the finances of the city of Prusa. His first impressions of Bithynia are then described. He has found there 'a spirit of obedience and loyalty which is your just tribute from the population'. He adds, almost as an afterthought: could a land surveyor be sent out to him? The reply is again sympathetic: 'I wish you could have reached Bithynia without any illness.' But then the tone becomes more official. 'The date of your arrival in Bithynia I have noted from your letter.' The imperial archives obviously noted the official date of entry into the province. Trajan then adds two further points. First: 'Your first task must be to examine the accounts of the various towns, as they are evidently in confusion.' Second: no surveyor will be sent. 'There are reliable surveyors to be found in every province and no doubt you will not lack assistance, if you take the trouble to look for it.' The letter is both courteous and succinct.

Once in post, the correspondence burgeoned. Should Pliny use public slaves as prison warders, or should soldiers be used? The latter would be more reliable but it would entail taking them away from their military duties. If a change were made, should anything go wrong one side might blame the other. He received a crisp reply: 'We should continue the custom of the province and use public slaves as warders.' He was reminded of the general rule 'that as few soldiers

Trajan was one of the most successful, militarily, of all the Roman Emperors, pushing the Empire to its limits. This included an area north of the River Danube (almost equivalent to modern Romania) which became the province of Dacia, for a short time only. The title was used later for a province to the south of the river. As a successful soldier, Trajan was commemorated by his column, which gives a detailed insight into the Roman army of his day.

as possible should be called away from active service'. Pliny could hardly have been surprised at such a reply from a soldier-emperor, who makes clear that Pliny has no discretion in this matter.

A great range of topics were referred to the Emperor during Pliny's tenure of office. Permission to rebuild the baths at Prusa: 10.23. The baths are old and dilapidated; the people are anxious to have them rebuilt. 'My opinion is that you could suitably grant their petition'. Trajan agrees, so long as the finances of the city are not strained. 'Provided no new tax is imposed and there is no further diversion of funds ... intended for essential services.'

Military postings: (10.27) 'Your freedman and assistant procurator Maximus,' writes Pliny, wishes to have an additional six soldiers to the ten Pliny had already awarded him on an earlier instruction by Trajan. Pliny adds that he had on his own authority given Maximus two mounted soldiers as an escort, since he was about to travel to Paphlagonia in order to collect corn. The Emperor agrees, then adds that when the mission has been completed the two soldiers Pliny has posted to the assistant procurator, together with the two the procurator has given him, should be enough. Obviously a military Emperor had a keen eye for postings commensurate with status.

Exemption from jury service: 10.58 and following. Should Archippus be exempt because he was a teacher of philosophy, or be removed from the register because, having broken out of prison, he had never completed his sentence? 'The case seemed to me to need your official ruling.' Pliny sends copies of earlier correspondence from Domitian and an edict from Nerva as background information to the applications for exemption he has received. He also gives additional background information in the text of his letter. Trajan replies that Domitian may not have known Archippus' position when the Emperor restored him to his former status. Furthermore, as the Prusians had erected a number of statues to him they must have known his history, but nonetheless honoured him. 'But none of this means, my dear Pliny, that if any new charge is brought against him you must not give it a hearing.'

Then there are questions about the status, cost and maintenance of foundlings: (10.65) Pliny has consulted the precedents, but could find neither a general rule nor a particular case that could apply to Bithynia. He describes his researches, but states he does not think he should be guided by precedents; instead he asks for 'an authoritative opinion'. Trajan replies that he can find nothing in the official files of his predecessors of any use. The question is about the status of free persons who were exposed at birth, but were then brought up as slaves by those who rescued them. 'I am therefore of the opinion that those who wish to claim emancipation on this ground should not be prevented from making a public declaration of their right to freedom, nor should they have to purchase their freedom by refunding the cost of their maintenance.' (10.66)

Sometimes imperial sensitivities overcome a real need. Pliny was visiting Nicomedia when a widespread fire broke out. People watched it without doing anything; furthermore, there was not a single fire engine in the town. Pliny ordered buckets and fire-fighting apparatus to be provided. However, this might not be enough: could not a fire brigade be formed, limited to 150 men? Pliny added he would ensure that only genuine firemen were appointed and their privileges not abused (10.33). This time the answer was brisk:

> You may very well have had the idea that it should be possible to form a company of firemen ... but we must remember that it is societies like these which have been responsible for the political disturbances in your province. If people assemble for a common purpose, whatever name we give them and for whatever reason, they soon turn into a political club.

There is to be no fire brigade. Pliny has done the right thing by already providing sufficient equipment. Property owners should make use of it themselves, while calling on the help of the onlookers. (10.34)

On the other hand there is an occasional lighter, even humorous touch. Pliny realised Trajan feared that the lake at Nicomedia would drain away if it were connected to the river. However, he believes he can resolve the fear. Details then follow. Trajan replies, 'My dear Pliny, I can see that you are applying all your energy and intelligence to your lake.' As the governor had worked out many ways of dealing with the problem, so Trajan concluded, 'You choose the way then which best suits the situation. No doubt there are experts in the province to carry out the works.' (10.61, 62)

Christians presented Pliny with a novel problem. He believes there is a policy involving their examination, but he has never been present at a formal trial (*cognitio*). He asks what is the nature or extent of punishments to be handed down, seeming to know that being a Christian is a punishable offence. He needs to know the grounds on which an investigation can be started, as well as how far it should be pressed. Should any distinction be made as to age or sex? If a retraction were made, should a pardon be given? Was mere profession of Christianity a punishable offence or had a crime to be alleged? He then goes on to describe what his practice has been when someone charged with being a Christian has been brought before him. He tells Trajan that he has asked them in person whether they are Christian. If they admit it, he then asks the question a second and even a third time, warning the accused of the punishment awaiting them if they still persist. If they remain obdurate they are found guilty and sentenced to death. There is nothing to suggest that Pliny had been pro-active against Christians, merely that accusations had been laid before him. However, he goes on, once he started to deal with the problem the charges became more numerous and varied, being accompanied by anonymous pamphlets in which persons were named. In cases which he thought right to dismiss because the accused denied being Christian, or asserted that they had abandoned the faith, he required them to demonstrate their loyalty by reciting after him a form of words invoking the gods, followed by an offering of incense and wine to the statue of the Emperor brought into court for this purpose. Thus an outward and visible sign of loyalty to the Emperor and Rome and its traditions was made. Pliny then goes on to describe how he had dealt with those whose names had been submitted by an informer. They were treated in the same way: an act of reverence to the statue of the Emperor and images of the gods, together with a renunciation of Christ. The number of people being brought before him, he remarks, was growing considerably and was likely to continue to do so; therefore he has halted further examinations until he receives imperial directions.

In reply, Trajan endorsed the steps Pliny has taken, but goes on, 'It is impossible to lay down a general rule to a fixed formula. These people must not be hunted down.' Pliny is not to be proactive. If cases are brought before him, then he must hear them. Those who make their position clear 'by offering prayers to our gods' are to be pardoned, however suspect their previous conduct may have been. Note that Trajan writes nothing about reverence to the Emperor; perhaps it was too obvious to need a mention. Finally, 'Pamphlets circulated anonymously must play no part in any accusation.' In brief, there should be no 'witch hunt'; everything should be done according to law, without reliance on anonymous informers and pamphlets. The touchstone is loyalty to the regime. Verbal and literary support for it, as in the letters of Paul and Peter, was not enough: there must be an external demonstration through the customary ritual (10.96 and following).

Pliny is assiduous in demonstrating not only his own loyalty, but that of his province. 'It is my prayer, Sir, that this birthday and many others to come will bring you the greatest happiness and that in health and strength you may add to the immortal fame and glory of your reputation by ever new achievements.' The response reads like a standard reply to similar messages that must have come in from all parts of the Empire. 'I write in acknowledgement of your prayers, my dear Pliny, that I may spend many birthdays made happy by the continued prosperity of our country.' (10.88, 89) 'We have discharged the vows, Sir, renewed last year, amidst general enthusiasm and rejoicing and made those for the coming year; your fellow soldiers and the provincials vying with one another in loyal demonstrations. We have prayed the gods to preserve you and the state in prosperity and safety and to show you the favour you deserve for your great virtues and above all for your sanctity, reverence and piety.' So went the dispatch of 3 January, reporting the New Year oath of loyalty. Again the reply seems stereotyped: 'My dear Pliny, I was glad to hear from your letter that the soldiers and provincials, amidst general rejoicing, have discharged under your direction their vows to the immortal gods for my safety and have renewed them for the coming year.' (10.100, 101)

No doubt Agricola in Britain, as well as governors elsewhere, sent in their letters. Perhaps declarations of loyalty were written in the same strain. Failure to carry out the ritual or report it would arouse suspicions. Unfortunately, we have no details of the correspondence between governors in Britain and the Emperors. Given his ideas about the regime, it is hard to imagine Tacitus reporting his father-in-law as using the same sort of language employed by Pliny. We are told merely that he wrote his despatches in a spirit of modesty and without laurel wreaths (*Agricola* 18, 39). Such a relatively low-key style may have been less risky than either boasting or, indeed, obsequiousness, given an Emperor of Domitian's temperament, but Tacitus implies it made little difference. The Emperor expressed delight, but was inwardly jealous. No evidence is adduced. Direct quotations might have enabled the reader to decide whether there was a common bureaucratic style of writing in the administration which governors were expected to use: Augustus certainly paid attention to a governor's style as a whole, as well as grammar and vocabulary. One man was relieved of his command for writing *ixi* instead of *ipsi*! Might Trajan's letters hint at an agreed idiom? Or did Pliny recognise better than some others how the ruler of an authoritarian regime preferred to be addressed?

There is another significant difference between the two governors. Pliny's role was essentially civilian: he was sent primarily to deal with a financial problem. Agricola was a military man: field operations marked most years. Civilian affairs were kept mainly to the close season. The appointment of a iuridicus indicated the need to ensure the dispensation of justice throughout the year. Agricola needed to be free to address a military programme.

He took the field immediately on arrival in Britain. The move against the Ordovices, even though the summer was over, seems to have had two elements. The first was to finish off an operation Suetonius Paulinus had been unable to complete on account of Boudicca's rebellion. The second was to assert authority after a period in which there had been not only unrest in Britain, but some disaffection in the army. Once these objectives had been achieved, Agricola was able to push north. His very presence, in strength, persuaded native peoples to accept Roman occupation. The third season brought him to the River Tay. Consolidation marked the fourth season. The fifth was marked by attention to the north-west of the island, south of the Clyde. The sixth consolidated the north as a whole. There were slight setbacks from time to time, from which he recovered, finally bringing the enemy into the field at Mons Graupus in the far north. It was the major battle of his governorship, and a decisive victory. Agricola had virtually doubled the size of the province. After this, pacification was needed: the mistake of Paulinus was to be avoided. The government had learnt the lesson, and the error was not repeated. Agricola showed himself to be as much an engineer as a field commander, enmeshing the conquered terrain in a network of forts and roads. Alongside this building programme, Tacitus tells us that as opportunity offered, or could be created, Agricola initiated a cultural one. Peace was made attractive. Tribes laid down their arms. Hostages were taken. The sons of leaders began to adopt the style of the new rulers. Romanisation was underway.

What resources did a legatus augusti have in an imperial province to discharge his military, administrative and judicial responsibilities? They had to be requisite for the tasks set before him; inadequate resources were likely to bring about their failure. Once he had these, then everything would depend upon the governor's gifts and capacities to manage them effectively. First, there were the troops at his command. The number of legions in the provinces is generally clear: four, then three in Britain, five in Syria. The ration strength of a legion was standard. Its technical sub-divisions are not always easy to discern, as we shall see later. In addition, there were auxiliary infantry and cavalry regiments. Their number in a province is not easy to calculate. At Mons Graupus, for example, Tacitus mentions the

Batavians and Tungrians at an early stage of the conflict. Thereafter he confines himself to 'other cohorts'. A governor was always able to contract the line of command, enabling him to deal directly with anyone or any unit as he judged necessary. Secondments and detachments from both the legions and auxilia would be required for special duties and operations, at the command of the governor. Sometimes the numbers could be considerable.

The governor also had to relate to the commander of the fleet, classis Britannica, even though its principal harbour was in another province, at Boulogne. The safeguarding of communications across the Channel was of vital interest to him. If the admiral were not a subordinate of the governor in Britain, nevertheless he would have to attend to any requests sent to him. Agricola seems to have been able to call up the services of the fleet as he advanced north. After Mons Graupus it was he, not the admiral, who ordered the ships to sail on, finally establishing Britain to be an island.

The Arch of Constantine in Rome is an example of the way in which some Emperors chose to mark their triumphs. Governors had to be careful not to interfere with imperial prerogatives, lest their careers be cut short.

Inscription on the Arch of Constantine: note the depth of the incisions.

Hadrian's Arch in Athens. There were arches of different kinds throughout the Empire, generally celebrating an Emperor.

Next, the governor had subordinates for civil government. Some of them would be soldiers allocated to a particular task; others would have been civilian personnel who might have entered office with the governor, or had been recruited locally. During the first two centuries this might have been easier in the eastern provinces than in the western tribally-organised communities, where Romanisation still had some way to go. Neither Pliny nor Tacitus gives details: the former merely mentions his staff; the latter tells us Agricola appointed the best men, refusing to use either freedmen or slaves for the transaction of official business. Nonetheless, the provinces did have public slaves. Pliny used them as prison warders. An inscription from London shows their presence in Britain. The wording shows them to possess some status (and wealth) more than being merely 'hewers of wood and drawers of water'.

The governor also had legates supervising regions in his province, as well as centurions for maintaining administrative relations with local authorities. They could have been men on secondment while on active service, or demobilised officers who retained their former rank. The ranking of a centurion is clear; that of a regional legate is ambiguous. At the annual meeting of the provincial council which brought together the leaders of the civitates, at least the legates may have been present as participating observers. While the council might be regarded as a ceremonial body convened mainly for renewing allegiance to the Emperor, it did give the governor an opportunity to gauge feelings in the province as well as make policy announcements.

A governor might well turn to his quaestor for advice on legal issues. However, from time to time the Emperor would appoint a iuridicus to relieve the governor of judicial responsibilities when he was heavily involved in other – often military – matters. Inevitably this legal officer had considerable autonomy, not least in sentencing. Whether a defendant could appeal to the governor after sentence or go straight to the Emperor is unclear. Probably, non-citizens were dealt with completely in the province. Citizens could appeal to the Emperor directly; a governor who interposed himself between the appellant, the iuridicus and the Emperor would need to feel very sure of his ground.

The iuridicus would need his own staff, probably appointed by him and brought by him into the province. Since the process was

PROVINCIAL ADMINISTRATION

MILITARY ROLES

	GOVERNOR, GOC	CO FLEET
	TRIBUNES	
CO LEGION	CO LEGION	CO LEGION
CO AUXILIARIES	CO AUXILIARIES	CO AUXILIARIES
CENTURIONS	CENTURIONS	CENTURIONS
OTHER RANKS	OTHER RANKS	OTHER RANKS

CIVIL ROLES

CHIEF JUSTICE : CIVIL AND CRIMINAL CASES AND APPEALS [a]

LEGATUS IURIDICUS: ARBITRATION RE ROMAN AND TRIBAL LAW

ROAD BUILDING AND MAINTENANCE: CURSUS PUBLICUS

SUPERVISORS OF CIVITATES

SUPERVISORS OF AREAS

SUPERVISION OF
CIVITATES   MUNICIPIA   COLONIA

PROVINCIAL COUNCIL
PROMOTION OF ROMAN CULTURE

PROCURATOR

TASKS:
IMPERIAL PROPERTIES, MONIES, TAXATION, IMPERIAL ESTATES

[a] All cases where capital punishment or condemnation to the mines could be involved.

Diagram 3

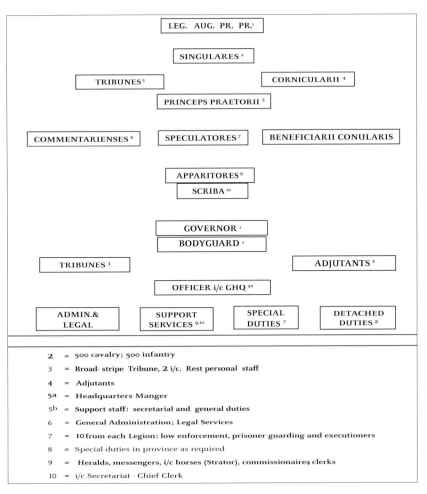

Diagram 4

inquisitorial rather than adversarial, not everyone on the staff may have been learned in the law. Literacy was perhaps more essential. Some may have needed the capacity to take shorthand. Indeed, both literacy and numeracy were essential for all departments of provincial administration: neither the office of the iuridicus nor the department of the procurator could have operated without them. The Vindolanda tablets indicate these skills were present, and not only in the higher ranks but at all military and civilian levels.

The governor also needed a good communications system, which the cursus publicus provided. The Empire had good roads, along which were official bungalows (mansiones) where accommodation and relays of horses were available for authorised users. Permits were not lightly given by the Emperor, lest the system were to be abused. Travelling over water might be more problematic, unless there were fast sailing packets. If sailing permits of some kind were available, the centurion bringing Paul to Rome did not have one, for he had to find what shipping he could. Even though the Emperor was the official dispenser of permits, there must have been some allocated for use by a governor. If there were not, the communications system would have been so unbalanced as to affect efficiency. Communications could hardly have been one-way traffic. Reports to Rome could not depend on chance modes of transport, nor could fast-moving situations hardly be handled well if couriers depended on whatever resources they could find. It is hard to believe that Suetonius Paulinus was unable to send official communiqués to Rome for lack of official permits.

A signalling system assisted communication: the heliograph in sunnier provinces; fires and smoke in duller climes. Whether any could span the English Channel is doubtful, except in rare exceptionally clear conditions. Flags were useful, but probably only over short distances. For anything more, relay stations would be required, either on promontories or from specially built towers. Full reports or appreciations of a situation were too detailed for transmission by signals. They were only suitable for brief commands, requests, or information. In any case, it would have been risky to send some messages *en claire*: official codes would be necessary. It is said that Tiberius could get a message from his villa on Capri to the signals HQ at Rome in two-and-a-half hours, no mean achievement, but that was in a climate more favourable than north Britain, where smoke and flame might be slower!

Finally, a governor had to take note of the presence of another imperial official in his province, but one who was not a subordinate. This was the procurator, who with his staff constituted a parallel executive system. The two roles crossed over executively only in the person of the Emperor and his ministers, but at a provincial level a working collateral relationship was highly desirable, since the procurator provided a service to the governor as the paymaster to the army. Periodically, the activity of one would cross over that of the other: we can glimpse something of that cross-over from an

The name on the tombstone of this governor of Pannonia Inferior found at Aquincum (Budapest) has disappeared, but the title of his role is given: 'Leg Aug Pr Pr' (legatus augusti pro praetore). The name of the dedicator is not given, but we are told he/she was happy to discharge this duty of commemoration and did so willingly: 'VSLM' (*votum solvit libens merito*).

inscription at Risingham, where a gate and adjoining walls were repaired by the First Cohort of Vangiones while Alfenius Senecio was governor, but the work was carried out under the supervision of Oclatinius Adventus, 'Procuratore Augustorum' (RIB 1234).

During the first century of the province of Britain there were subordinate rulers who possessed some autonomy, but over whom a governor would be required to keep a watch. Later, these were phased out. Under Septimius Severus the unitary province was divided into two: Britannia Prima with its capital still in London, and Britannia Secunda with a new capital at the legionary fortress of York. Diocletian carried this reform further by subdividing many provinces, almost doubling the number. Britain was broken up into four provinces; there may have been a fifth later. This change could have resulted in the employment of civilians in roles hitherto occupied by the military. The sources of their recruitment may have been twofold: from the Empire as a whole, and the British provinces in particular, but it is hard to discern the balance. It depended on the literacy and numeracy of civilians in any province. The hierarchy of accountability also became more complex: a governor, now known as a praeses, was accountable to the vicarius of Britain, who in turn was accountable to the praetorian prefect in Trier and, in his turn, to an Emperor, one of the four Emperors when the Empire was organised in that fashion. When there were four, then accountability would be to the Emperor of the region allocated to him. The latter was a more radical reform than the former, because it removed military responsibility from the governor and vested it in generals. It was the first step in restraining over-ambitious governors, who, if they commanded a considerable force, could make a bid for power, as Albinus had done in Britain. However, the civitates and colonies seem to have continued much as before, but provincial councils could have multiplied and yet, as a possible appeal to Honorius implies, be in touch with one another as the occasion required.

been on active service he would have been stationed at Herod's court in Tiberias, along with the cohort posted to the tetrarch as a mark of honour from the Emperor. If he were a liaison officer, Tiberias was, again, the most likely base for his work.

Some inscriptions demonstrate the procuratorial cursus. Titus Haterius Nepos began as the prefect of a cohort, followed by a posting as a military tribune; he then became a prefect of cavalry, which may have been combined with duty as a census officer, both activities being in Britain. Thereafter he moved to be procurator of Greater Armenia, after which he was responsible for the ludus magnus, then for inheritance matters, the census, petitions, after which he became prefect of the vigiles and finally prefect of Egypt (ILS 1338). Another man, Laco, whose full name is lost, had been prefect of the vigiles and procurator of the Gauls, i.e. of more than one province. During the rule of Tiberius, Aquitaine was linked with Narbonensis, though the latter was a senatorial province: the imperial writ could transcend boundaries. Lugdunensis may also have been linked with Belgica. These may have been temporary arrangements made as the provincial administrations were set up. From the time of Domitian, however, the practice was formalised, with the role designated officially as the procuratorship of Belgica and the two Germanies, located at Trier. It was an appointment that was generally the stepping stone to higher things. There were probably other procurators with a narrower responsibility, to supervise the annona (grain), together also with raw materials necessary for the maintenance of the Rhine armies. The procurator of Lugdunensis had charge of the quadragesima Galliarum, a 2.5 per cent duty payable on goods entering the three Gauls. Normally, the procurators concentrated upon the direct taxation system (tributum and stipendium), leaving the publicani to deal with indirect taxes (vectigalia), but the procuratorial staff calculated the amount due from the peoples based on the results of the census. In Gaul, Augustus supervised one in 27 BCE, followed by Drusus in 12 CE and Germanicus in 14 CE. Belgica was also broken down into smaller units, each of which had its own procurator. Their appointment might have been to a particular tribe, though sometimes the territorial boundaries are not stated. If these men were the leaders of their local communities, the appointments were unlikely to be marked by efficiency, in which case beneficiarii might be sent to tighten up the administration (see below). There were internal taxes, like the portorium exacted on goods crossing certain frontiers – defined not for protection, but for revenue purposes. In the second century CE publicani came to be replaced by conductores – wealthy individuals on whom the duty of collection was imposed.

The procuratorial salary scale is given on another inscription. Sextus Varius Marcellus, a beloved husband and father, was procurator of the aqueducts, with a salary of 100,000 sesterces; procurator of Britain at 200,000; then procurator of the private account (rationis privatae) at 300,000. He went on to become vice prefect of the Praetorian Guard and of the city (of Rome); then a senator (vir clarissimus); also prefect of the military treasury; commander of Legio III Augusta; and finally governor of the province of Numidia. His career as a whole should perhaps be considered exceptional, since he was married to a niece (clarissima femina) of the empress Julia Domna, wife of Septimius Severus and father of Elagabalus. (CIL x.6569)

Other procurators, and at least some of their assistants, were recruited from freedmen and slaves drawn from the imperial *familia*. One subordinate, Naevius, was stationed at Bath. He raised an inscription not only for the welfare of the Emperor, but to state that he had been responsible for the restoration of the principia. The inscription also implies the presence of regional administrative offices located throughout the province. (RIB 179)

There could be great attention to detail in order to prevent tax evasion. The procurator of Neapolis, in Egypt, reported that, by sampling, a cargo of wheat had been found to be adulterated. He therefore instructed the strategos of the dispolite nome to make up the deficiency from the sitilogoi who had shipped the wheat, to which he added supplementary charges and additional costs as the penalty for defalcation. Not content with issuing the command, he ordered a report to be made to him when the appropriate account had been credited. (P. Oxy. 2125 & 708)

Boudicca's rebellion gives some insight into possible tensions between the governor and the procurator. On the death of the client king of the Iceni, Prasutagus, he bequeathed his realm in his will to the Emperor Nero. Officials of both the procurator and the governor descended on the Iceni. There was plunder, pillage, servitude and rape. For this mismanagement, Decianus Catus must bear considerable responsibility as procurator. With the governor, Suetonius Paulinus, campaigning in north Wales and the failure of Petillius Cerialis to suppress the resultant rising, when an appeal for aid was made to Catus his response was to send two hundred badly trained armed men. Already unpopular, he fled the province as the rebels moved south, destroying the old capital, now a colony of veterans at Camuludonum (Colchester).

Paulinus had to break off his campaign against Mona (Anglesey) to march south, gathering forces as he went. He decided to abandon London and Verulamium (St Albans), through which the rebels then marched. Calleva Atrebatum (Silchester) may even have been reached, since recent excavations show serious damage by fire inflicted about this time. Communications with the continent could be endangered. At worst, the province could be lost. The situation was compounded by the refusal of the praefectus castrorum (acting commanding officer during a vacancy) of Legio II Augusta to move out of Exeter to join the main force. Paulinus was clearly on the defensive; he was, however, an experienced and successful general.

The statue of Boudicca in her chariot, brandishing her weapons, is a modern one. The leader of a major uprising against the Romans in the first century CE has become the icon for brave Britons resisting the threat of a foreign invader.

In 41 CE he had campaigned successfully in Mauretania, and was the first Roman to cross the Atlas Mountains with a force. Later, in 69 CE, he was to support Otho, taking a leading part in the campaigns round Bedriacum. As the crisis developed after the suicide of Otho, he threw his weight behind Vitellius, whose death probably also ended his own career, as Vespasian came to power.

Choosing his battleground carefully, he won an overwhelming victory against the rebels. The follow-up was at least as harsh as the events which caused the rebellion. A punitive policy was prosecuted, where even unconditional surrender seemed insufficient; punishment seemed to continue without end. Meanwhile, a new chief procurator, Julius Classicianus, had arrived to replace Decianus Catus. Classicianus, having grasped what was going on, came out in support of the defeated rebels, who were on the verge of starvation as winter approached. Tacitus suggests he was motivated by dislike of Paulinus; that may be, but it may have been more to do with the tensions always possible when two separate executive systems cross and neither has authority to override the other. On the other hand, Classicianus may have concluded that Paulinus' remorseless reprisals after victory would reduce provincial revenues, for which he was accountable. This was true: they needed peace to recover. An adverse report went to Rome, as a result of which Paulinus was loaded with honours – after all, he had saved the province – but was recalled to face an enquiry into the loss of some ships.

A change of governor also required a change of policy: pacification must be the aim. It was in the imperial interest. The *mandata* must surely have laid this down – the inference seems justified. The actions of Petronius Turpilianus, who succeeded Paulinus, showed him as both more flexible and milder, contenting himself with quelling the turbulence but no more. In itself this was significant, for it gave the province a necessary period of repose. His successor, Trebellius Maximus, was even less active; affability replaced action. The result was rebellion, this time by the army. No blood was shed, but the governor remained in office, rather than in power, placating the army and thereafter being largely dependent on their sufferance. Vettius Bolanus, the successor of Maximus, receives the same treatment by Tacitus, who may be somewhat unfair to him since he admits that Bolanus did at least try to win over the provincials, which suggests a continuing policy of pacification. Indeed, the purpose of these passages in the *Agricola* may have more to do with rhetoric than with actual details. The representation of a succession of governors as decent but ineffectual serves to prepare the reader for the entry of the decisive, energetic men, Cerialis and Frontinus, followed by Agricola, the great man who did more: not only restoring effective control of the army, but by deploying it in the field doubled the size of the province; he then brought peace and reconciliation through the redress of grievances, followed by a programme of Romanisation.

The title of procurator came to replace that of praefectus during the latter part of the first century for the governance of smaller provinces like Judaea, Noricum, Thrace and the two Mauretanias. Pontius Pilate, in office in 33 CE, is described as praefectus on the inscription found at Caesarea. By the time the first gospel was written about 67 CE, as well as the later three, he is described as procurator. In most cases these governors were drawn from the equestrian order, exercising full military, civil and judicial authority.

Finally, a place should be found for the role of the beneficiarii. They were to be found in both the gubernatorial and procuratorial systems, though not fitting easily into the hierarchy. They were men designated for special duties, which could be either short- or long-term, recruited from the army among ranks below the centurionate. What is significant about them, however, is that their rank took second place to the authority they derived from whoever appointed them: so we find beneficiarii who are consularis, procuratoris, legatus legionis, and so on. The inscriptions they erected give little indication of their tasks, generally stating no more than to whose staff they belonged. Presumably they were sent out according to the needs of the appointing officer, but having regard to their curriculum vitae, the tasks allocated to them ought to have been proportionate to their experience and capacity. Their powers of discretion were probably limited, but their ability to observe and report back was likely to be important. With the authority conferred upon them they could be a crucial influence, whose words could not easily be set aside.

CHAPTER 6

CLIENT KINGS

Early in the occupation of Britain, while Aulus Plautius was governor, Tacitus informs the reader, 'Certain states were granted to Cogidubnus as king; he remained most loyal up to the time I myself can remember. It is an ancient and long established practice of the Roman People to use even kings as instruments of enslavement.' They were regarded as Friends of the Roman People (*Agricola* 14).

We are not told the names of the states (tribes) over which he ruled. His realm may well have been a specific creation. The very name Regnenses suggests this could well be the case: peoples over whom he ruled. Tribes were not fixed entities, inasmuch as one clan might be either a sub-section of a major grouping, as with the Setantii in Brigantia, or be absorbed for whatever reason into another tribe. Cogidubnus' name on an inscription suggests considerable delegated authority: he is king and imperial legate (regis legati augusti is the language used), and he carries a praenomen, nomen and cognomen (Tiberius Claudius Cogidubnus). Such status and authority conferred so early in the history of the province also suggests he was known, favourably, to the imperial authorities. Tacitus could remember his loyalty down to his own times. We may reasonably infer that he demonstrated it before the invasion as well, indicating the presence in Britain of something more than casual trading contacts in the period between Julius Caesar's forays and Claudius' invasion. His high status and authority seem to be confirmed by the buildings at Fishbourne. It is a pity the inscription mentioning him is displayed in a street wall in modern Chichester, for there is no inscription on the extensive site stating who built the complex, for whom, and why. Had it been the summer residence of the governor, surely there would have been some statement, including the name of the Emperor of the time. The anonymity is puzzling. All things considered, Cogidubnus is the most likely occupant.

An inscription of the times in honour of Claudius, erected soon after the invasion, declared that the Emperor received the submission of eleven kings, probably tribal chiefs to the north and west of the territory first conquered (ILS 216). Whether they were honoured as clients, allies, or just subjected to direct rule we cannot tell. We do know, from later events, that the Iceni of Norfolk and the Brigantes, covering a large area of the north, were client kingdoms. When Prasutagus, king of the Iceni died, he bequeathed his kingdom to Nero. Evidently either he could not, or judged it inappropriate to, hand on his authority to an Icenian heir. Cartimandua ruled as queen of the Brigantes. When she was succumbing to a coup led by Venutius (her husband, but not king), the Roman army was sent in to uphold her (*Agricola* 16, 17). Of the nature of the rule of these British kings we have no exact knowledge. To perceive what a client king might do, we must look to Palestine.

Over the centuries the country had been part of a number of empires. By the time of the Maccabees (second century BCE) a high degree of autonomy had been secured, strengthened by a treaty of friendship and mutual assistance with the Roman Republic. While the high priest may be regarded as the head of state, real power lay elsewhere. Antipater was the dominant force until his death, when he was succeeded by his two sons: Phasael was captured by the Parthians and later committed suicide; Herod was the other. He fought back and lived.

Born in 73 BCE, he had become a Roman citizen (47 BCE), and when attacked by the Parthians he fled to Rome for protection (40 BCE). Mark Antony nominated him king of the Judaean ethnarchy. His position was further strengthened when the Roman army stormed Jerusalem to secure his position when it was under threat. He remained faithful to Antony throughout the war with Augustus. His patron's defeat at Actium left Herod in a vulnerable position. He took a bold step: facing Augustus, he did not deny his previous allegiance, but swore that he would serve the victor with the same devotion and loyalty he had displayed for the defeated general. The victor was persuaded, and confirmed Herod in his position; indeed, more was added when, as Augustus, he added to his realm cities that Pompey had freed in times past (30 BCE). Iturea was added later (23 and 20 BCE). Herod was indeed a client king, regarded as a friend of the Emperor and of the Roman people. The Jews were under his direct rule, not that of the provincial administration.

He proved himself an able administrator, though suspicious, impulsive and cruel; murders and assassinations occurred throughout his rule. The economy was developed. Caesarea Maritima, with its artificial harbour, was built and named after the imperial house. The second temple was built by him to support the Jewish religion, but he separated the spiritual from the temporal function and made his own nominations to the high priesthood. A programme of Hellenisation was carried out, both in architecture and life style. Above all he

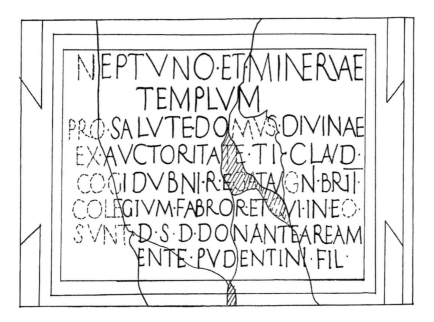

Cogidubnus. This inscription throws light upon local Roman government. The status of Cogidubnus as a client king is made abundantly clear: note the careful description of all his titles. He is associated with the large building complex at Fishbourne, but the inscription is to be found in the wall of a building in Chichester.

promoted the imperial cult: there may not have been sacrifices to the Princeps, but there were rituals on his behalf. Herod's loyalty to Rome was unwavering. He was able to recruit his own gentile army and maintain a secret police. Not surprisingly, order was generally maintained throughout his territories, even though orthodox Jews did not regard him as one of their own since his family hailed from Idumea, beyond the traditional Biblical southern boundary of Judaea. They loved the temple he gave them, but not the donor.

This brief survey enables us to perceive what a client king could and could not do. There was considerable discretion in all domestic and internal affairs, as long as loyalty to Rome and its ruler was constant and unequivocal. A client king risked foreign wars at his peril; a satellite's action might involve the Emperor as an unintended consequence. Both diplomatic initiatives and an independent policy could incur imperial disfavour. Military defensive actions were permissible if a king were under threat. Herod probably took more risks than Cogidubnus, yet both survived. Had either of them ever overstepped the imperial mark, almost certainly we should have heard of it.

The story of the visit of the Magi, whether historical or not, indicates the political dangers which could be caused by religious enthusiasm. They did not only come from beyond the Empire, but from a state with which the Romans had a fractious relationship. On arrival in the client kingdom, they asked its king about someone else who might well supplant him as the true king of the Jewish people. At best this could be regarded as tactless; at worst it was dangerous for all concerned, since the position of Herod and his Emperor could be threatened, to say nothing of the Magi themselves. The security of Herod's own position as a client king depended on his ability to control the Jewish people by keeping them loyal to the Emperor; any pretender needed to be disposed of. The later story of the massacre of young boys could be interpreted as a pre-emptive strike to cut down anyone who might undermine not only his own position, but that of the Emperor to whom he had sworn allegiance (Matthew 2.16 ff.). If the story is regarded as more symbolical than actual, few would argue that the action of Herod was untrue to his character and grasp of *realpolitik*.

In brief: client kings appear to have had a relatively free hand to govern in the domestic affairs of their kingdom, but foreign policy and military forays beyond their frontiers were beyond their authority. Further, in domestic affairs tribal laws and customary practices do not seem to have been abrogated. Roman law was for Roman citizens; other inhabitants were treated according to the laws of the civitas to which they belonged.

With the death of Herod (4 BCE), his client kingship ended. It fell to Augustus to decide what do. He continued the practice, but divided the territory of the father between the three sons. Philip took the north, Herod Antipas the central region, and Archaelaus the south, all with the title of tetrarch, not king. Philip ruled quietly until his death. Herod Antipas did the same, while moving his capital to a new site which he named Tiberias, after that Emperor, following the example of his father at Caesarea. In 36 CE Tiberius involved him in his negotiations with the Parthians, which showed a degree of confidence in him on the part of that suspicious and inscrutable ruler. In 37 CE Aretas of Nabataea invaded Herod's territory, because the tetrarch had divorced his daughter in order to marry Herodias, his niece. Roman reprisals were only halted by the death of Tiberius and the succession of Caligula, who was asked by Herod (prompted by Herodias) for the title of king. He fell on a bogus charge of treason brought by his nephew, who impugned his uncle's loyalty to Rome. Caligula, ever suspicious, deposed Herod Antipas and awarded the state to Herod Agrippa, the nephew, again with the title of tetrarch.

Herod Agrippa shows the degree of intimacy that had grown up between the imperial house and his own family. He had lived at the imperial court until the death of Drusus (son of Tiberius). Claudius added Judaea to his realm, but then became suspicious of Agrippa's ambitious plans and the client kingship was brought to an end with his death (44 CE).

The acute problem lay with Archaelaus. He was in repeated dispute with the Jewish community leaders, who exercised their right of appeal to the Emperor by asking for his removal and the introduction of direct Roman rule. (They had previously asked for direct rule earlier, on the death of Herod). In the end, Augustus acceded to their request: Archaelaus was deposed, sent into exile at Vienne in Gaul, and a prefect appointed in his stead. By the time the Christian gospels were written, the word used for governorship had become procurator. The change from prefectus neither changed the role content nor affected the right of the native provincial leaders to appeal directly to the Emperor.

We can see something of the way in which the internal administration of such a province operated, especially in the dispensation of justice, by considering the case of Jesus of Nazareth. He was a subject of Herod Antipas as tetrarch of Galilee, but was arrested in the province of Judaea. The Jewish authorities in Jerusalem who had instigated the operation proceeded to deal with him there. Ecclesiastical historians have argued about the legal process, not least as to whether Jesus had a proper trial before a properly constituted court. In one sense, this does not matter; what is clear is that he was examined inquisitorially by Jewish leaders with a view, apparently, to producing a capital charge that they could bring before the procurator. He was not to be accused of a breach of the peace in the Temple, nor for heresy or disobedience of the Jewish law. The charge was disloyalty to Rome as a pretender to kingship. It was a capital charge, if proven, where the sentence was death. It must be heard, not by the native leaders but by the procurator. Here the line was drawn between local and provincial authority.

Brought before Pilate, the governor discovered Jesus to be a subject of the tetrarch of Galilee, and in one tradition referred the case to him. Herod Antipas, who happened to be in Jerusalem, declined to take up the offer: the trial should take place where the alleged offence had been committed. Thus he signalled his own loyalty and deference to the provincial administration. Pilate therefore heard the case, coming to the conclusion that the prisoner was not guilty. However, two factors impeded the dismissal of the charge. First of all, the prisoner refused to plead. What was the presumption he should make on that account? Playing safe, Pilate proposed to let him off with the Roman equivalent of a caution: a light beating. This proved to be unacceptable to the prosecution, who then played their trump card. They told the procurator, 'If you set him free you are no friend of Caesar's; anyone who makes himself king is defying Caesar.' (John 19.12) They affirmed their loyalty to the Emperor, to whom they could appeal directly, as they had done in the past, complaining of Pilate's faulty administration. They implied the disloyalty of the procurator. Evidently a governor could be manipulated. The rest of the reported dialogue displays the sarcastic defensiveness of a man whose career might be in danger (John 19; Mark 15.6–15).

In ordinary internal matters, the government would not intervene. At Corinth, Paul held regular debates in the synagogue in an endeavour to convert both Jews and God-fearers to Christianity. Severe disputes broke out, as a result of which Jewish community leaders sought to bring Paul to trial before Gallio, the proconsul of Achaia. Their charge was: 'We accuse this man of persuading people to worship God in a way that breaks the law.' There might be a loophole in the law here. If they could persuade the proconsul that Paul was promoting a cult not recognised by the government, then he might punish him. However, Gallio thought the charge related to the observance of Jewish law. He threw the case out as soon as he heard it: the defence was never called. 'If this were a misdemeanour or crime I would not hesitate to attend to you but if it is only about quibbles and names and about your own law, then you must deal with it yourselves. I have no intention of making legal decisions about things like that.' (Acts 18.11–16) Internal problems in societies and cults do not seem to have come within the provincial purview. Criminal cases would be a different matter.

When Paul was arrested during a riot in the Temple, his treatment was quite different from the treatment accorded to Jesus. A military detachment broke up the riot and took Paul into custody (Acts 21.32, and chapters following). To appease the mob, the officer in charge was about to command Paul to be flogged, but the centurion asked the tribune if he knew what he was doing since the prisoner was a Roman citizen, with all its rights and protection. The military action and enquiry were stopped in their tracks as the officer realised he could be charged with assaulting a citizen. He started another enquiry as to Paul's supposed offence, including a conference with the Jewish authorities. After it, Paul was brought in to face his accusers, the provincial officers having withdrawn. The hearing ended up as a shouting match laced with verbal abuse. The army intervened to remove Paul from the room, and the meeting broke up. Paul was despatched from Jerusalem to the provincial capital at Caesarea, where the case could be dealt with before the prefect. The tribune, as the arresting officer, handed in an account of all that had transpired in Jerusalem, and the case went forward. Paul's Cilician origins were not taken into account; there seems to have been no question of sending him to Tarsus. Roman law dealt with citizens *in situ*, not by original domicile. Felix proceeded with the trial but it was not completed before he was recalled, to be succeeded by Festus, who decided to begin all over again. A further trial followed, during which Paul was asked whether he would consent to the case being transferred to Jerusalem for adjudication there, presumably by the Jewish authorities. Refusing the offer, he is reported to have said, 'I am standing before the tribunal of Caesar and this is where I should be tried ... I appeal to Caesar.' To which Festus replied, 'You have appealed to Caesar; to Caesar you shall go.'

Later, when Herod Agrippa spoke to Festus at the end of a supplemental hearing convened to enable the prefect to submit the appropriate documentation to the central authorities, he remarked, 'The man could have been set free if he had not appealed to Caesar.' The appeal of the citizen overrode the authority and opinion of the local government (Acts 24–26). What happened to Paul thereafter is unknown. Probably he suffered with many other Christians as scapegoats of Nero after the great fire of Rome.

Unfortunately, we have no comparable knowledge of the way in which Cogidubnus conducted the internal administration of the Regnenses, nor what were the details of his role as imperial legate. From his titles we may infer that he loyally promoted the imperial cult, but there is no direct evidence of his doing so. It is by the accident of Christian history that we can gain some insight into the regime of client kings. They were a relatively short-lived political device, but served their purpose during the early days of Empire; by the end of the second century they had been phased out.

CHAPTER 7

EGYPT

Egypt was in a provincial class of its own. For long an important kingdom with its own distinctive government, for some centuries it had also been the centre of the Ptolemaic Empire. For Mark Antony, the opponent of Octavianus, it had been a powerful resource as a result of his alliance with its queen, Cleopatra. Victorious at Actium, Octavianus marched on to crush them and the kingdom. Both died, probably by their own hand. Caesarion, borne by Cleopatra of Julius Caesar and a possible rallying point for opposition, was murdered soon afterwards. Egypt lay at the victor's feet. The kingdom was turned into a province in which special measures were taken to prevent any phoenix of opposition ever raising its head again. There would be no client king here.

Octavianus, now Augustus, appointed a praefectus aegypti, of equestrian status, as governor. No senator or prominent equestrian was allowed to enter the province unless he possessed the express permission of the Emperor to do so. It was to be a closed country: the personal estate of the Emperor, whose principal function was to supply annually one-third of the grain needed to feed the city of Rome.

The old kingdom possessed a long-standing administrative system. This was not abolished; instead, a Roman superstructure was imposed upon its internal organisation. Some titles were retained, and where they were not there may have been a change of role content. Military functions were separated from civilian; one role became two. The

Ptolemaic division of the country into districts was retained: there were thirty of these, known as nomes. The senior officials were Romans, and the rest were drawn from the native population. Egypt's long-standing culture had provided a cadre of civilian administrators. Translators were required for the transaction of public business. The official language was Greek, but the native language was necessary in many departments.

The nome was governed by an official known as strategos (a Greek term). They were grouped in threes, to be supervised by an epistrategos located at Delta, Heptanomia, Arsinoite and Thebaid. All were Roman equestrians, and appointed by the prefect. Each had his capital in the metropolis of the nome. The strategos was assisted by a subordinate known as royal secretary, the Ptolemaic title being retained for this role.

In the administration of justice, most people came before the strategos. In the courts, Egyptian laws enshrined in custom and practice obtained, though in fact much was Greek in origin. In common with the governors of other provinces, the prefect went on circuit to dispense justice in major cases as well as those without precedent. Alongside this activity, the prefect also carried out an inspection of the local administration in the districts through which he passed. There could also be direct orders. The prefect wrote to the strategoi of the Heptanomia and Arsinoite nomes, 'I have already in a previous letter ordered you to conduct an industrious search for bandits.' (This was a chronic problem.) He continued, 'I do not regard this task of secondary importance, but am in fact offering rewards to those of you who cooperate ... You will be liable to penalties as well as risk of dismissal if any malefactor commits an act of violence and goes undetected.' He added that soldiers had been dispatched to the districts to ensure their peace and security by not only pursuing bandits but also 'suppressing incipient raids' (P. Oxy. 1408).

There were a number of Greek cities in the province: Nankratis (in the Nile Delta), Ptolemais (Upper Egypt), and Alexandria, which was also the provincial capital. Hadrian added a fourth – Antinoopolis, in memory of Antinous, his friend, whose untimely death caused the Emperor long-lasting grief. Known as poleis, these cities were autonomous, with their own constitution and privileges like the towns of the Decapolis (Ten Towns) in Palestine. Those who qualified as citizens were enrolled in tribes and demes (townships). Residents who were foreigners might have no entitlement; slaves did not, since they were regarded as a thing (*res*), not a person. The boule was the elected city council. For more than two centuries Alexandria had no such body, on account of its hostility to the conquering Augustus.

There were a number of important roles in them. The gymnasiarchs managed the gymnasium, normally at their own expense, providing oil for lighting and massage. The kosmetes trained young men (ephebes) in the rituals there. The etheniarch supervised the grain supply. The agoranomos managed the market. The archierus presided over the religious rituals of the city. The exegetes was the chairman for the year of the committee managing the administration of the city. As in the rest of the Empire, holders were expected to bear the expenses of office themselves. The provision of games and administration could be financially burdensome: Aemilius Stephanos found he had been nominated by Aurelius Amois 'as being of sufficient means and eligible to succeed him in the office of collector of money taxes due from the villagers of Sinkepha'. This he thought unreasonable, and not in keeping with the sharing of compulsory public service, known as a liturgy. 'I, therefore, resign my property to him in accordance with the imperial ruling.' Some men preferred to surrender their real estate to the nominator in order to have him perform the liturgy instead. Septimius Severus ordered that those who did so should suffer no diminution of status, with its attendant privileges (P. Oxy. 1405).

Egypt also contained a significant number of Jewish communities. For centuries, the Ptolemies had conferred significant privileges upon them: one-fifth of Alexandria was allocated to them. They had their own ruling committee of elders, and along with the Greek cities and Romans, they were excused the poll tax, which fell upon the men of the nomes. These privileges the provincial administration maintained for the Jews, until the first- and second-century revolts in Palestine undermined imperial confidence in them. The ethnic complexity of cities, particularly in Alexandria, resulted in area segregation. This, however, was not enough to prevent the outbreak of periodic serious riots, which often did considerable damage, since they took time to quell.

There was a major army garrison within the province with two legions, one stationed at Alexandria and the other at Babylon, near

Memphis. In addition, there were auxiliary units as well as a naval squadron, whose anchorage was also at Alexandria. Besides routine garrison duties, soldiers were detached to mines, quarries, frontier posts, road junctions, and supply depots for grain. They could remain in service after demobilisation: Publius Juventius Rufus, formerly tribune of Legio III and prefect of the mines of Mount Berenike, was director in chief of the emerald and topaz mines, and the production of pearls and all the mines of Egypt. Indeed, at the end of their engagements soldiers would settle in the province, marrying local women, to live the ordinary life of a civilian. As we shall see later, the government regulated the status of both the partners and their children when there were mixed marriages. Along with the Vindolanda writing tablets, the papyri of Egypt open a window on to the lives of the provincials, as inscriptions throw light on the organisation which provided the sinews of provincial administration: the Roman army.

CHAPTER 8

LOCAL GOVERNMENT

While the government of the Empire was authoritarian, it was not highly centralised. Within the provincial structure there was a good deal of subsidiarity. Local government was strong. In the Hellenised area of the east, it was based a good deal upon the old Greek city state; in the west, tribes were used. The administrative structure of a province held the local frameworks together. The central government in Rome managed overall security, commanded the army, controlled taxation and determined foreign policy. Local authorities managed local markets and finance, together with council elections, as well as law and order within their territories; the latter within well-defined limits. The provincial administration appointed officers who had a 'watching brief' to oversee, as well as liaise with, local communities in the imperial provinces. They were not primarily executives, but no doubt there could be interventions, should they be judged necessary. It would be hard to reject their 'advice'. Councillors, particularly the duo viri, could also turn to these officials for advice, probably in grey areas lying between the provincial and the local spheres of government. In some cases, however, a single magistrate (magister) might be appointed instead. Whether this was a temporary or permanent appointment is unclear; however, it might be a useful office during a transitional period from a tribal structure to the establishment of a civitas.

As we have seen, the government continued to use the administrative system they found operating in Egypt. A supervisory framework, staffed by Roman personnel, was imposed upon it to ensure final control by the provincial and central governments.

We are relatively well informed about the local government structure of the city state of Athens, which can be set alongside the *Politics* of Aristotle. During the time of the Roman Empire, the general pattern obtained in many provinces which were city states in origin and Hellenistic in culture. The smaller states had been grouped into larger provinces, but common features remained. Members of these units were used to a degree of autonomy in administration, centred upon the council (boule) and its membership. It was generally located near or by the agora (in Latin, forum), which was an open space used for markets and surrounded by a number of public buildings. Within the limits of the urban unit would be found sanctuaries, one of which might hold the municipal archives, while another might act as the treasury. There might also be a store for grain, a reservoir, a gymnasium, and baths, together with a library and theatre. Stoas (colonnades) were also to be found, used for a variety of purposes ranging from social gatherings to education. Justice would be administered from the bema, an open-air tribunal, but there might also be a law court housed within a building. Finally, there would be a number of temples dedicated to a variety of gods, not least one dedicated to the patron of the city and another to the imperial cult of Rome and its Emperor. For all these functions officers were needed, but the organisational structure was not dissimilar from the civitates of the west: a council, councillors and officers fulfilling specific roles (P. Oxy.).

In scale there was probably nothing to compare with the size and diversity of all this in Britain. Nonetheless, the basic urban layout and administrative structure was much the same. Venta Silurum (Caerwent) may have only been 44 acres in extent, with a forum of no more than 260 by 182 feet, but built on a compact rectangular base, walled in and entered through an archway, were to be found the council chamber (ordo/curia), tribunals, taverns, a snack bar, and shops – one of which may have been a health salon, as the presence of nail clippers, ear scrapers and tweezers may indicate. The columns of the basilica were of the Corinthian style, whereas those of the stoa poikile in Athens were Doric on the outside and Ionic on the inside. There does not seem to have been a library, but probably there was entertainment, given the apparent presence of taverns and bars. There were also the public baths, which were as much a social centre as a washing place, well described by Seneca in one of his letters, where he describes the vendors making their way through the gossiping crowds. Both he and Marcus Aurelius regarded them as unsuitable places for philosophers, believing they should shun the throng, for they could return home as lesser persons than when they went out.

The forum at Silchester (Calleva Atrebatum), covering two acres, was much larger but still conformed to the same basic shape: an open square lined on three sides by porticoes, shops and offices. On the fourth side stood the basilica, 234 by 58 feet, whose superstructure was supported by two rows of Corinthian columns. At either end were tribunals for the dispensation of justice. At the west end of the basilica stood the marble-lined curia. There were baths and temples nearby. Though few, if any, cities could match the democratic Athens of old, nonetheless something of the same kind of administrative structure may have been operative throughout the Empire; local self-government based on councillors and committees. A description of organisation cannot convey anything, however, of the vitality of the life of the communities they served. To sense that, we must turn to Pompeii. There, more than 2,500 posters have survived in the form of graffiti painted red or black on any suitable surface, showing that there were elections. The posters imply both campaigning and canvassing. The texts are generally restrained: 'Please elect Popidius Secundus as aedile, an excellent young man.' There may have been agreed billboard sites, since the texts for current elections are often painted over from earlier ones. Sometimes a poster may have been defaced during a campaign: 'If you meanly blot this out, I hope you catch something nasty' seems to indicate dirty tricks campaigns, employing character smears as well as black counter-factual humour. A list of female supporters painted up outside a bar may indicate no more than the preferences of the barmaids, but it could also be negative propaganda by a candidate hinting that his opponent depended upon the support of lower-class people, perhaps even slaves. Who would welcome the support of The Late Drinkers, or The Pickpockets? If these posters were humorous, the pilloried candidates were not likely to have seen the joke; attempts to discredit them would be a more likely interpretation. Some posters indicated group support: the millers, grape pickers, fishermen, whether as a guild or informal association. All this implies contests: public, honourable maybe, but also with a dark side; elections here were not merely a formality. Electioneering was energetic, though the electorate was much smaller than the resident population since foreigners, slaves and women were all excluded. The voting system may have been by groups rather than by individuals. The traditional Roman system was to divide the electorate into sub-groups; these may have been defined in ways other than by districts. In a large city like Rome, tribal units may have been used, or occupational associations may have been employed. Whatever was the organisation, the result would have been to make a choice from however many candidates were on the slate. The collected group votes would determine the electoral result.

We need not assume that the council was made up of independents or divided into formal political parties any more than we assume a voting system based on individual votes cast. First, we should remember the extent of patronage in Roman society: the relationship between patron and clients was very important. Electoral influence may have been in proportion to the number as well as the status of clients. In the same way, a businessman may have had political influence from both his wealth and number of employees. If the former were used for public benefit, this too would help in an election campaign. When Jucundus posted up a notice declaring the quality of his bread, we may interpret the graffito as more than a statement of value. The oblique reference is to his supply and management of the bread dole in the city, from which, no doubt, many benefited; but it also showed to everyone his public spirit, making him worthy of support. Voters could infer the largesse would continue if he were to be elected.

Local officials and councillors were unpaid, but were expected to fund public affairs like games and festivals, as well as the erection (and, no doubt, repair) of public buildings. If a significant number of clients were necessary in order to succeed in local politics, then candidates needed to reveal the depths of their purse alongside the probity of their character. The first two requirements could be demonstrated with relative ease. The revelation of good character was more difficult; an opponent might impugn it by innuendo. A poster stating that X had the support of runaway slaves could make the voter wonder what sort of a man was being held up to ridicule.

The remains of Pompeii put flesh and blood on the politicians of the city. Unfortunately, we have no such description from Britain. The tribes of the west were completely different entities from the towns of the east.

Before the advent of Rome, they operated in a different way: first of all, their head might be called king or chief; whatever the term employed, he was regarded as the father of the tribe, exercising by right unquestionable power. He was the head of the family, the chief of chiefs. There was a strong hereditary element in the succession, not necessarily from father to the eldest son but the one judged most suitable at the time. If no man were thought suitable, then someone from another family would be considered. There were members of the ruling family who were also called chieftains: they had their own territory, founding sub-groups known as septs. Below this rank were all those who claimed descent from earlier chiefs, or kinship with the present ruler. At the lowest level were the commoners, who for one reason or another – they may not always have known how or why – were members of the tribe. To them fell the menial tasks such as herding. In battle they would very probably be stationed at the rear of the formation. Devoted loyalty to the chief was paramount, not individual private opinion. This is not to say the chief behaved dictatorially. The indaba or tribal assembly was influential; it was probably made up of the chieftains of the septs or head men within the tribe, along with the chief priest(s) or shamans. Issues were talked through, for as long as it took, until there was a consensus wherever possible; only if the debate failed might the father of the tribe make a final decision. The abandonment of this structure and its replacement by elections for a council, combined with a regular rotation of officers, was something quite foreign to the tribes. It was a radical change, needing something more than a provincial decree to make it effective. At the least an organised induction would be needed. This is where the local legates and centurions might have had a crucial role. One major issue was the role of the chief. Did he stand aside to become a ceremonial figure while others assumed his governmental role as duo viri? Or did he stand, to be joined by a junior member of his family? Were they elected repeatedly? It is easier to see the chieftains becoming decurions as the indaba turned into a civitas council. While they knew how to discuss, they might have needed some training in the duties of aediles. The paternalism and lack of individuation in a tribe may have made the transition to Roman-style local government long, slow and difficult. In the end, it appears to have succeeded. Given the titles of Cogidubnus, we can hardly imagine he was vulnerable to a vote conducted by his subjects. We may also assume that neither Cartimandua nor Prasutagus had to stand for election. The chiefs may have been reduced to honorific status as the regime of client monarchs was phased out.

We have no knowledge as to whether they were consulted about any redrawing of tribal boundaries that took place, or the relocation of a capital. The provincial officers may have dictated that, whether in ignorance or after investigation we cannot know. A *fait accompli* was probably most likely: it is hard to think tribal leaders had a veto over such decisions.

There is little to suggest that tribal structure and practices changed much over time. It is not unreasonable to consider what occurred in the Anglian kingdom of Northumbria in the seventh century, when Edwin was the chief of chiefs. An indaba could be called at any desired location; the chief did not necessarily have a fixed capital. He chose York to decide whether Christianity should be admitted into the tribe. The chieftains and head men gave their opinions, which were capped by the speech and dramatic action of the chief priest, who clearly perceived the sense of the meeting.

Matters may have been different in colonies of veterans, like Gloucester, where the residents made up self-governing local government units composed of Roman citizens and their families, who may well have experienced the structure, perhaps before joining the army. The constitution of these colonies was based on that of Rome itself. The bonding that could have taken place after many years of military service, together with the many non-military tasks the men had carried out, may have aided the administration. There was a considerable body of experience here to be drawn on, which must have aided local government.

A municipium operated in much the same way, with a constitution based on the Latin allies of Rome. It might be much more a commercial centre than a governmental hub. They were cast widely throughout the Empire. Unfortunately, only one is known in Britain: Verulamium (St Albans). There ought to be more!

Whether we write of a tribal civitas, a colony or a municipium, the actual form of organisation was much the same. There was the constituency for producing, by whatever process, the councillors (decurions), the council (ordo or curia) and its officers. Of these, the aediles bore much of the heat and burden of the day; in fact, they were the sinews of local government, responsible for every aspect of management: market days, the arrangement of stalls, health and safety, the upkeep of buildings, supervision of the water supply, road maintenance and, indeed, anything which was for the good of their community. Aediles were managers, not artisans. Day-to-day labours, ranging from the simplest tasks like street cleaning to the sophisticated such as maintaining financial records, might well be discharged by public slaves. We should also bear in mind that officials had responsibilities beyond the capital: there was also a considerable hinterland of villages, hamlets and farms, all of which required supervision. It was where councillors had their own estates, which could serve as a power base for their standing in the community. Inevitably they had power in their own communities. Above them in the hierarchy, and with final control, were the duo viri – the two men who constituted the chief executive. They presided over the council as well as acting as justices and, finally, having the oversight of the administration of the civitas as a whole. Once every five years there were duo viri quinquennales who enrolled new members of the council, together updating the electoral register. This was, perhaps, the local government position with the highest status. They might expect deference, to say nothing of solicitations when the review was pending. These officers would normally have served as one of the duo viri, and might well have been aediles before moving up into the role. With a term of office limited to one year, in a small civitas the turnover of men might be limited; some could have been returned regularly over a number of years.

Most forts in the military zone of Britain, north and central Wales, together with England north of the Trent, had civil settlements which grew up outside the walls of the forts. Housesteads is a good example. These canabae appear to have had no separate, formal constitution. Whether residents fell within the authority of the civitas in which they were situated is unknown. Given soldiers having off-duty dwellings in these settlements, civilian administration centred upon a tribal capital some distance away may have given way to the de facto management of the nearest commanding officer. However, there may often have been some kind of community association, as an inscription set up by the civilian residents at Vindolanda would indicate (RIB 1700).

The civitates of a province like Britain were also required to send representatives to the annual meeting of the provincial council. The size of the delegation is not known, but it is likely to have been more than one man. The duo viri are the most likely officials to have made their way to the provincial capital; perhaps tribal chiefs could attend. This meeting can sometimes be dismissed for having no executive function. This misunderstands its function; councils are consultative bodies rather than executive instruments. They should not be underrated. First of all, the civitates were able to reaffirm their loyalty to the Emperor; the regular declaration of commitment to him was of no small importance, as we saw from Pliny's correspondence. Second, the central and provincial governments could use the opportunity to make policy announcements. Third, the governor, with his staff, could gauge the temper of the provincials. And finally, the meeting gave representatives the opportunity of networking outside the plenary sessions. Some problems, like a grey boundary area, might be solved on such occasions without going to full trial before the governor, who would, of course, have to authorise an informal agreement before it could take effect. We should also consider the possibility of the centurions of the civitates, as well as area prefects, attending the council, whether as participants or observers. In the last resort a council might appeal to the Emperor, as seemed evident from the reply of Honorius telling them to look, henceforth, to their own defence; nothing was going to come from the central government. An individual civitas or similar local government unit might exercise the same privilege as did the Jews on more than one occasion, of appealing to the Emperor. Roman provincial administration is noteworthy for the extent to which it practised subsidiarity, whereby the day-to-day administration of local units, whether of towns or civitates, was placed in the hands of their leaders, with provincial officers supervising them, dispensing justice in cases referred to them and providing security. Local government units probably lacked an official police force as much as they were without a fire brigade, but at any rate, in parts of Britain a military unit was never very far away, to be called upon in an emergency. In provinces without garrisons, the military establishment of a pro-consul or procurator might be sufficient to deal with local disturbances. If all else failed, then the central government would have to send in additional troops. The *pax Romana*, however, seems to have allowed people to go about their business generally unarmed; indeed, there were times when the carrying of weapons was forbidden. When the Empire started to totter under the impact of foreign invasions, some provincial inhabitants were said to have lost the capacity to defend their own communities effectively: disarmed by peace, they had become over-reliant on the army. The government had wanted a quiet, obedient, disarmed population in the provinces. They got it; but the price in the long term may have been communities lacking both the skills and the resilience to fend off raiders and intruding settlers. As the provincial administration disintegrated, the wheel came round full circle. Roman local government was replaced by tribal units not dissimilar to those existent in Britain before it ever became a province of the Empire.

That is to look forward some centuries. Throughout the occupation, and especially during the earlier years, there must have been a constant problem of communication between the native peoples and the Roman administrators. It was one thing for the government to reorder local government, but quite another to be able to carry it out; in the longer term, if the local leaders did not speak Latin and the Romans did not speak the local language, what kind of communication could take place? Translators must have been necessary, but where could they be found, especially in the early decades? Not in Britain on arrival. Hostages, refugees and tradesmen from Britain resident on the continent in the virtual hundred years after the invasion of Julius Caesar could have produced a pool of people who were bilingual. The connection between tribes like the Belgae and Parisi, with sections resident on both sides of the Channel, yet in contact with each other, may also have provided not only translators but intermediaries who could, for example, negotiate the surrender of the tribal kings to Claudius without bloodshed. Because the governor, his officials and senior army officers were not permanently stationed in a province (only in rare cases would they know the local language), throughout its history Roman provincial administration must have depended upon the services of translators. Local leaders needed some Latin, if only to understand orders; speaking it correctly would be more difficult – vocabulary probably triumphed over grammar. It must have been acquired by gesture and practice. When the government of a province at all levels is studied, one is driven to conclude that linguistic Romanisation was a *sine qua non* of administration; baths, togas and Roman culture in general were secondary, dependent on rulers and ruled being able to communicate with each other.

CHAPTER 9

THE ROMAN ARMY

The Roman Army was a formidable fighting force. On its loyalty, in the last analysis, rested the security of the Emperor. Augustus had not only recruited a good many legions and auxilia but, on his path to power, had paid them himself. Once he was undisputed ruler they were carefully nursed. The failure of the army of Germany to swear the oath of loyalty in January 69 CE signalled a year of four Emperors. Armies putting up their own Emperor resulted in clashes between opposing forces, marked by short-lived regimes. Septimius Severus had grasped this political reality when he advised his son to attend to the army and leave the others alone.

The army, however, was much more than a fighting force upon which the regime rested. The legions in particular provided a pool of skilled men who occupied a number of significant roles in what today would be regarded as civilian activities. Our concern here is not with military prowess, but with the army as a resource for the provincial administration. Soldiers were detached for special duties; army records show how varied and considerable these might be. A report on the ration strength of the auxiliary First Cohort of Tungrians stationed at Vindolanda stated the number of absences to be forty-six as guards for the governor, at Coria (Corbridge) 337, a number at places not now decipherable, and sick and wounded thirty-one, making 265 out of a total strength of 752 available for active service. The end of that active service did not necessarily bring a return to private life: men could be transferred to a range of tasks in the provincial administration.

Within a legion of 5,000 a number of skills were to be found: agrimensores (surveyors), plumbarii (lead smiths), specularii (glass workers), aerarii (bronze smiths), carpentarii (carpenters), scandularii (roof makers), ferrarii (blacksmiths), lapidarii (stone masons), aquilices (hydraulic engineers), fabrii (craftsmen, possibly concentrating on the making of bricks since fabrica indicated a brick factory), architectus (master builder), and polliones (millers). All of these were, of course, primarily military roles, but they were also useful in civil enterprises. Such skilled soldiers were likely to be immunes, excused routine army fatigues and with the status of principales.

After the army had passed through an area, the occupation would be consolidated by the building of forts, first of all perhaps in turf, but later, when conflicts had much diminished, in stone. Later still, when the government judged areas to be pacified, forts could be decommissioned. Thereafter the sites could be handed over for civilian use. In a province conquered but relatively recently, soldiers with the appropriate skills could be seconded, both in order to modify the existing buildings and to construct the new. Whether it were a green field site or a programme for converting military premises, the erection of large public buildings like a forum, market area, law courts, basilica, temple and baths all required considerable skills in construction. It was labour-intensive work for which local labour might be used, but would need both technical supervision and general management. Some tasks would need to be done by the troops themselves. Decisions about the execution of such projects would be a matter for the provincial officials and army commanders, who would be concerned not to impair the primary military role. A great deal would depend upon the situation at any one time. Whether everything could be carried out directly by whole units would depend on the nature of the project, together with a judgement by the high command about how many men could be spared for such work.

Later, local councils might take the initiative. The town of Bougie (Bejaia) in Caesarean Mauritania, during the reign of Antoninus Pius, wished to build an aqueduct, but could not find anyone competent to execute the work. They applied to the governor for help, and he supplied them with a librator (surveyor) from Legio III Augusta. Under his direction an aqueduct of 21 kilometres was produced, which included a tunnel of 428 metres. Timgad, north of the Aures, was built entirely by the military on the order of Trajan. Its influence seems clear, since it was initially laid out as a square of 350 metres. Britain does not provide us with this degree of detail, but there can be little doubt, for example, that Corinium (Cirencester) was built on the site of a fort when the tribal capital of the Dobunni was moved there. The legionary fortress at Glevum (Gloucester) was turned into a colony for the veterans of II Augusta when the legion was moved to Isca (Caerleon-on-Usk) in the territory of the Silures, whose capital was at Venta Silurum (Caerwent). The army was very probably at work in the former, and may have profited from military assistance in the latter.

The military were also responsible for building roads, one of whose principal purposes was, of course, facilitating troop movements, together with the delivery of the logistics on which the army depended, but there would also be civilian traffic. Alongside them, the army could also be responsible for mile-stones. Elsewhere they may have erected or supervised the erection of boundary markers. Land to be registered would also be surveyed, its properties and necessary thoroughfares marked out. Such functions required skills for which the army was often the only source of manpower in a province.

LEGIONARY COMMAND STRUCTURE

LEGATUS LEGIONIS ──────────────────── HQ STAFF
MESSENGERS = CORNICINES
TRIBUNUS LATICLAVUS [CAVALRY]
ADMINISTRATIVE
TRIBUNI ANGUSTICLAVI STAFF   CLERK
TESSERARIUS
PRAEFECTUS CASTRORUM EAGLE BEARER = AQUILIFER

COHORT I SENIOR CENTURION	COHORT II CENTURION	COHORT III CENTURION	COHORT IV CENTURION	COHORT V CENTURION	COHORT VI CENTURION	COHORT VII CENTURION	COHORT VIII CENTURION	COHORT IX CENTURION	COHORT X CENTURION
OPTIO	OPTIO	OPTIO	OPTIO	OPTIO	OPTIO	OPTIO	OPTIO	OPTIO	OPTIO
5 DOUBLE CENTURIES	6 CENTURIES	6 CENTURIES	6 CENTURIES	6 CENTURIES	6 CENTURIES	6 CENTURIES	6 CENTURIES	6 CENTURIES	6 CENTURIES
20 Tent parties	10 Tent parties	10 Tent parties	10 Tent parties	10 Tent parties	10 Tent parties	10 Tent parties	10 Tent parties	10 Tent parties	10 Tent parties

UNIT ROLES	RATION STRENGTH		
Craftsmen			
Architectus	1 Legatus Legionis	1	
Mensor	1 Tribunus Laticlavus	1	
Hydraularius	5 Tribuni Angusticlavi	5	
Nanpegus	1 Praefectus Castrorum	1	
Ballistarius	10 Centurions (80 in a century)	10	
Specularius	10 Optios	10	
Sagittarius	5 Double Centuries in 1 Cohort	= 800	
Haruspices	110 Tent Parties of 9 = 480 x 9	= 4320	
Medici	1 Tesserarius	1	
Capsarii	1 Eagle Bearer	1	
Maginifer	120 Messengers & Administrative Staff	120	approx. 5268+
	plus unit specialists – see Unit Roles		

Diagram 5

The man dressed as a Roman soldier is a reminder of the fact that the security of the Emperor depended upon retaining the support of the army. Later in the third century the army, whether in the provinces or in Rome itself, became the political power broker. But whatever happened in the capital, the provincial administration remained heavily reliant on military personnel for the exercise of rule.

Administrative tasks were also undertaken by the troops. Reference has been made already to Rufus, who was in charge of the mines of Egypt. Men also conducted censuses, under the supervision of the governor. In the second century there was a censitor Brittonum Anavio(nensum) in Colchester. It was detailed work. 'Gaius Vibius Maximus, Prefect of Egypt, declares: The house by house census having begun, it is necessary for all persons who for any reason are absent from their home districts be alerted to return to their own hearths, so that they may complete the customary formalities of registration.' In tribal areas, that might mean returning to the tribal capital (cf. Luke 2.1–6). Clearly, the army facilitated the administration of the provinces.

Military establishments were also beneficial to the local economies. Once in service, a civil settlement was likely to come into existence. People moved in to provide goods and services; this stimulated crafts and commerce. A market might be brought into existence; if it flourished, the settlement might become a recognised centre for the production of pottery or metal goods, if the local garrison outsourced armour manufacture and repair. A leisure industry could also develop, with a tavern or two, laundresses, batmen and women, to say nothing of prostitutes, all serving off-duty soldiers who might well have their own dwellings in the village in which their partners and children lived. This seems to have been the origin of the thriving civil settlement at Vindolanda. The remains of the canabae at Housesteads can still be seen (complete with the inn, under whose floor a stabbed body was found, hinting at an incident that got out of hand).

Not all legionary veterans retired to the colony of their unit, nor did demobilised auxiliaries always return to their native land; instead, they might settle permanently in the province where they had served. Some might live in the settlement beside the fort where they had been stationed, where, too, perhaps, they had a house, family and friends. Others may have gone further afield, perhaps to the local tribal capital where, after settling in, they took part in its social and political life as decurions on the town council, and perhaps later as one of the duo viri. Settling in an indigenous community was probably an effective means of Romanisation, just because it led to an intermixture of ordinary peoples and stimulated an informal acculturation of generations, so as to modify life styles towards some

Roman practices in the process. Many a community would have welcomed an ex-soldier, not only on account of his skills but for his ability to speak and write Latin. He might also be numerate as well, and so help in the management of municipal finances. Once fluent in the local language, they could be useful as translators when local leaders had to deal with provincial officials who themselves might find bilingual veterans a help in the transaction of business. If the local legionary legate were respected, he might become patron of the town, willing to give the community an advocate who could be helpful at a time of need. The erection of an inscription paying tribute to a senior officer, as the Silures did at Caerwent, at least indicates some kind of viable relationship. On the other hand, there might be problems. A serving soldier in Egypt wrote a note of caution in his letter of recommendation to his demobilised brother, on behalf of Terentianus, 'an honourably discharged soldier'. The recipient was asked to acquaint Terentianus with 'our villagers' ways, so he is not insulted'. Marriages with local women needed regulation. 'If a Roman man or woman is joined in marriage with an urban Greek or Egyptian, their children follow the inferior status.' 'Egyptians who, when married to discharged soldiers, style themselves Romans are subject to the provision of status.' May we assume this rule to be applied throughout the provinces? It would be odd for Egypt to be unique in this respect. The process of Romanisation may be ambiguous in such circumstances.

There were other tasks to be performed where military and civilian roles were closely mixed: for example, all movements through Hadrian's Wall were controlled by the army. Soldiers must have acted not only as security officers but as customs officials, which was to be expected on the frontier. If a community were recalcitrant in paying its taxes, a centurion could descend upon them as exactor tributorum to ensure compliance. If there were boundary disputes, a soldier could appear as iudice dati to settle them. Other men might act as security agents or confidential couriers acting as diplomatic envoys, delivering messages between governor and Emperor. They were known as frumentarii, which suggests that originally they had something to do with the grain supply, as men who needed to move freely about the Empire, thus being less likely to arouse suspicion. Men given the status of beneficiarius were deployed on all manner of work, so wide-ranging that it cannot be easily described. A beneficiarius was someone sent on official business who took the rank or status of the person who sent him. The beneficiarius consularis was the authoritative representative of the consul; so was the beneficiarius legati propraetore of the governor. Procurators also used beneficiarii, who appear as beneficiarii procuratoris. Ex-soldiers who were enjoying a second career on the procurator's staff were designated beneficiarii or stationarii; they were attached to two principal officials. A governor's establishment could possess up to sixty, a procurator's ten, commanded by a centurion. Pliny was made aware of the need to keep the numbers within bounds (*Letters* 10.21). Beneficiarii might be sent to get grain, or to act as tax and customs officers. They could have ordinary police duties controlling rivers, roads and markets; we must not be too rigid in describing the roles of such men. No doubt there were official staffing figures for military and civil roles, but some discretionary power must have been vested in both governors and procurators to act at will, as extraordinary situations required. If it were not so, protocol could have deprived the administration of effectiveness. They, too, were the sinews of government.

Finally, the importance of the army as a cultural agent can hardly be over-emphasised. It was probably more effective than anything else in the provinces where troops were stationed. Important as its contribution to the provincial administration certainly was, the interaction between the lower ranks and the local population could be remarkably effective, sustained as it was over long periods. Men came into contact with local tradesmen, craft workers, innkeepers, through the services they offered. Perhaps their contact with women was the most important of all. Casual liaisons could become partnerships which were recognised as marriages upon demobilisation. By such means Roman governance could become accepted. Subsequent generations could consolidate the position, enhancing Romanisation through the passage of time.

This Romanisation was effective in a variety of ways at different social levels. One province might vary from another. Those of long standing, into which families had moved at a relatively early stage, could provide distinguished leaders like Trajan and Hadrian, who became Emperors. Their life style in such provinces was probably not very different from those described in the metropolitan literature of the times. In other provinces, architecture, amphitheatres and theatres, as well as pottery, might be more significant than literature. But where ex-auxiliaries settled in the area in which they had served, banquets, togas and Virgil would be absent; native pottery and house style would be largely unaltered. The families of former soldiers might well have had some workaday Latin. Only with the passage of time, and perhaps movement into major urban units, would the adoption of more Roman practices have been brought about. Yet even this modest level of Romanisation over three or four centuries could establish a sense of *Romanitas* that could be transmitted beyond the collapse of the west. Romanisation and commitment to Roman ideals were strong enough to influence the new regimes which succeeded the provincial administration. In some cases the commitment was sufficient for many to emigrate beyond the River Severn, or to what is now Brittany.

POSTSCRIPT

The instability of the Empire during the third century, as local regimes rose and fell and Emperors came and went, seemed to threaten the administration of empire. Not the least of these problems lay with the power of the army to set up and destroy Emperors, together with the capacity of some provincial governors to achieve a de facto independence, if only for a short time. Carausius ruled Britain and part of northern Gaul. There were frontier wars against such tribes as the Alemanni, Sarmatians and Saracens, together with a number of others, alongside a serious revolt in Egypt. In fact, there was civil war. Diocletian, who proved to be a great organiser, created Emperor by his army in 284 CE, instituted radical reforms. Some lasted for centuries, to shape the organisation of the kingdoms that arose from the disintegration of the provinces of the west. The changes were made at the highest level. The Empire was divided into two: east and west, each with its own Emperor, supported by a junior known as a Caesar, who was expected to succeed to the senior appointment on the abdication of their Emperor. Of itself, that did not affect the internal administration of the provinces. They were, however, profoundly affected by the subdivision of the provinces into smaller units. The number was doubled: that may not have affected the internal governmental structure – the separation of functions did. Governors, now known as praeses, had judicial, financial and general management functions. Their military role was removed, with the armies now being commanded by equestrians with the titles of dux and comes. This must have affected the internal administration; for example, if military personnel were withdrawn, this required their replacements to be civilian, some of whom would have to be drawn from the indigenous population, who could only be effective if they had the necessary competences of literacy and numeracy, which in turn depended upon the degree of Romanisation which the administration had achieved over the previous decades or centuries. No doubt some officials were posted in from appointments held elsewhere, but we should not assume that shorthand writers, filing clerks and others ranked in the lower levels of the hierarchy were drafted in. The provinces were grouped together into larger units known as dioceses, supervised by vicarii, who were themselves accountable to the praetorian prefect who was the deputy of their tetrarch. The levels of accountability were multiplied. Provincial authority was so subdivided: Roman provincial administration had become more complex, almost inevitably requiring an increase of staff. The provincial administrators, together with their superiors, were also confronted by a new taxation system which required appropriate administrative competence and a requisite level of numeracy.

The tetrarchy proved to be ephemeral, as a single entity was restored under Constantine. With the further passage of time, a division between east and west came about. The administration of the former held out; the structure of the latter gradually fell apart as provinces were raided and then occupied by peoples beyond the frontier, whose organisation was quite different from the Roman. Raids may not have undermined the structure and staffing of the provinces; settlement did. The incomers were tribal, with their own laws and customs. They may not have constituted the majority of the population, but they had overall military control. They might impose their will upon the provincials as they wished, or they might allow them to live according to their own laws; much depended upon the strength of negotiating positions. Further, if contact had been lost with the central government, or become highly erratic, and if senior officials were not replaced or no salaries were forthcoming for either civilians or soldiers, then the provincial administration would break up, as men had to find some means of providing for themselves and their families. Some may have found other work; others may have been taken into the service of the new rulers.

However, a number of the new rulers had some experience of Roman life and ways, having been in military service or living at court, possibly as hostages. Some at least had an awareness of the life and organisation of the provinces. For example, Theodoric was well versed in Roman administration. He maintained much of Roman administration in his kingdom: civilian affairs were in the hands of the Romans, military among his own people. Odoacer had served as a senior officer in the Roman army, and even received the approval of the Senate. Vortigern held much of Britain together during the dark period following on from the imperial rescript informing the British provinces that they should manage their defence, and by implication their own government. He successfully recruited mercenaries, who had some initial successes. Whether the provincial administration held together is another matter; the evidence is mostly lacking. Such evidence as there is indicates that a provincial capital like Cirencester was somewhat run down, but that may have been more economic than administrative, though the viability of the latter much depended upon

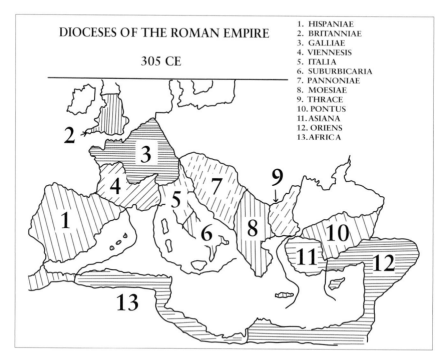

DIOCESES OF THE ROMAN EMPIRE

305 CE

1. HISPANIAE
2. BRITANNIAE
3. GALLIAE
4. VIENNESIS
5. ITALIA
6. SUBURBICARIA
7. PANNONIAE
8. MOESIAE
9. THRACE
10. PONTUS
11. ASIANA
12. ORIENS
13. AFRICA

Diagram 6

old provincial centres, where they were assisted by presbyters and deacons, some of whom had pastoral responsibilities in the hinterland. These churches fostered a sense of community by assisting vulnerable people like widows, orphans and refugee slaves with food, clothing, and even employment. A local church was not only a refuge but a provider of practical aid, which would be important after ruinous plundering raids which devastated whole areas. The bishop had both the status and resources to carry out work which in times past would have fallen to the provincial administration; for example, building programmes and the maintenance of irrigation systems, as well as the capacity to bring particular needs to the attention of the new rulers. These dioceses were grouped into larger units still, probably based on a regional capital, where a metropolitan, a senior bishop, was to be found. At each level there would be a synod at which policy and administrative issues were thrashed out, along with doctrinal clarifications. Above all these, from the sixth century, there were the patriarchs, a number of bishoprics accorded both a primacy of honour, as well as a jurisdiction, in the adjoining territories and in the Church as a whole. They were Jerusalem, the city of the crucifixion and resurrection; Alexandria and Antioch, cities of theological study; Rome, the old capital; and later Constantinople, regarded by the others as something of a parvenu. The Arab-Muslim invaders of the seventh century who conquered much of the Middle East and North Africa debilitated the patriarchs of Jerusalem, Antioch and Alexandria, making them more the leaders and protectors of the Churches, together with indigenous populations. The same applied to Constantinople, especially after it fell to the Turks in 1453. Rome alone remained, but even it suffered from the tribal invasions of the west, coming periodically under the sway of the new rulers. No further patriarchates were established in the west; there were more pressing matters to be dealt with. Additional patriarchates would have been a luxury, adding no significant resources to the struggle for survival. In any case, the new rulers were too jealous of their authority to concede an important part of it. The Roman pontiff could have honorific status. He could crown Charlemagne, but he would still appoint his own bishops. He, not the Pope, would bring Alcuin to his court, for both kings and the Church had a resource unknown to the imperial provincial administration: monasticism. Abbeys became cultural centres of learning with the study of great texts, preserved and produced by the production of manuscripts, while still providing hospitality to travellers and others in any kind of need.

The countryside was different: here the Church was more dispersed, sometimes dependent upon a room provided by a local landlord, whether in his house or in one of his properties in a village on the estate. Even here, however, contact of some kind was maintained with the diocesan centre. Either someone from the congregation would walk in to bring back the Eucharist to the congregation or a presbyter would come from time to time to celebrate the Eucharist among them. A by-product of these interchanges was to bring human needs to the attention of the deacons, who could assist with practical works of mercy, perhaps with the provision of a garment or pair of sandals.

If town and country were put together, a unit co-terminous with a civitas or province could be discerned. The bishop in Cirencester seems to have been related to Britannia Prima, the bishop of London with Maxima Caesariensis. Support for this view comes from the instructions Pope Gregory gave to Augustine as the programme for his mission to England in 597. The organisational structure was to be based not on the model of Diocletian, but of Septimius Severus. The Church was to be divided into two provinces, with a bishop based in London and the other at York: the old capitals of Britannia Prima and Britannia Secunda. London was to have twelve bishops as his suffragans, and so was York. These twenty-four bishops were probably to be based on the old civitates. The scheme was to be brought into operation gradually as the mission proceeded, but it was never completed. London failed to accept Christianity sufficiently to become the seat of a metropolitan. Canterbury took its place, as the original base of the Augustinian mission. The north of England never acquired its twelve bishops. As Caledonia became Christian Scotland disputes arose, as a result of which the land north of the Tweed received its own independent jurisdiction.

By the end of the fifth century, the Roman provincial administration as it is described here had passed away, but its structures were reincarnated in the Church as well as in, at least, parts of the new kingdoms on which present-day Europe has been built. Roman law has exercised its influence through the centuries to our own day. Latin remained the language of scholarship and diplomacy for centuries; it helped shape the romance languages we know today. The vocabulary of administration still draws upon the terms of Roman provincial administration, besides that of the central government. The Napoleonic Empire, the constitution of the United States of America, even the architecture of the legislature, bears witness to the rule of Rome.

The prosopographical studies of many scholars have made possible this outline of Roman provincial governance. There are lacunae: gaps we shall never fill in, in all probability. The description, no doubt, has simplifications, implying an orderly system. A caution should be entered: roles and role relationships are approximations, varying in their degree of accuracy to actual situations in which they were operative. There is an apparent formal structure, but there are exceptions, not always known to the historian any more than is the operation of the informal system. Organisational structures are held in the mind rather than on wall charts. There is always an element of ambiguity in the system. We can only judge by what we know of the outcomes.

In conclusion, we should not assume that the formal descriptions always operated in that manner, *in toto*. People in organisations make assumptions about what the formal position means; they may be right or wrong about them. The penalty for misjudgement could be severe. There is nothing to suggest that the term of office for a legatus augusti pro praetore was three years: we conclude it to be about that from a study of individual careers. The extension of Agricola's term may be a vote of confidence in him, or no more than a convenient ad hoc arrangement determined by a range of factors assessed by the Emperor and his advisers. His recall need not be interpreted as an adverse judgement upon him; quite the contrary: he served what amounted to a double term. We cannot discover what individual assumptions were; we can only observe what role occupants appear to have made of them. They have to be measured by the experience of living with the extant position. Governance is a correlation of what is formal, assumed and extant. Effective leadership in an organisation depends upon making an accurate assessment of how things actually are.

In an authoritarian regime, the supremo is not generally constrained by formal structures, with their definitions of boundaries or precedents. There will always be an overriding prerogative, dependent on the will of the supreme governor. Thus the legate in Syria could find that the Emperor had appointed a relative to be supreme commander in the province, to deal with a particular issue. The governor of Britain found he was recalled because of a judgement made about his policy. Officials in Roman government, whether central of provincial, held office at the will of the Emperor: there was no security of tenure. There was no way of removing an Emperor who lost authority because, for whatever reason, he lacked the necessary gifts and capacities. The office holder needed personal power to make his authority effective. If, as a result of a failure to harness power with authority, an Emperor lost the support of those about him (and in this case, the senior army officers), assassination was more likely than survival as a figurehead. The structure of Roman provincial administration seems well organised, and indeed there was some stability, but it was of role content; role occupants were dependent upon the will of the Emperor. They could change; the roles did not.

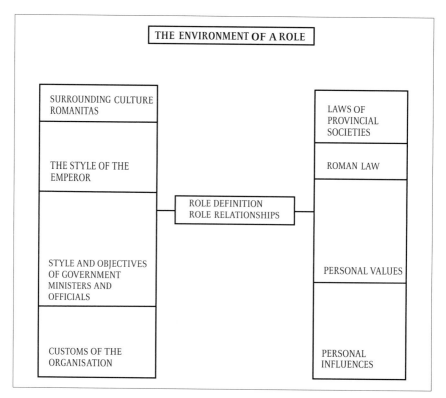

Diagram 7

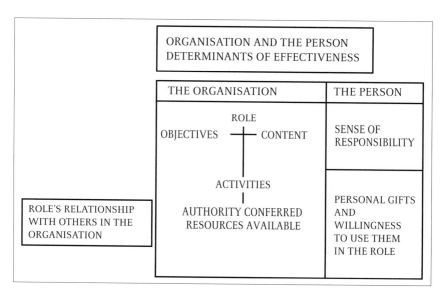

Diagram 8

GLOSSARY

ab epistulis	Role of chief secretary to the Emperor. Office holder: a senior equestrian procurator.
a censibus	Role of senior official, assisting in conduct of the census. Office holder: equestrian.
adlectus	A man enrolled into the Senate.
advocatus fisci	Role of treasury counsel. Office holder: junior equestrian procurator.
aedile	(i) Role of a senatorial magistrate. (ii) Role of a magistrate in a town, with general administrative duties.
aerarium militare	The military treasury based in Rome. Duties included the payment of bounties (gratuities) to demobilised soldiers (veterans).
aerarium saturni	The state treasury, located in the Temple of Saturn in Rome.
agens in rebus	Agent of affairs. Role of secret policemen in later Empire.
agens vice praesidis	Abbreviated to AVP. Role of acting governor.
ala	An auxiliary cavalry unit, either 500 or 1,000 strong.

a libellis	Role of an official dealing with petitions. Office holder: a senior procurator.
angusticlavius	Status of someone entitled to wear the narrow stripe.
a rationibus	Role of official responsible for accounts. Office holder: a senior equestrian procurator.
archon	Role of chief magistrate in Athens.
asiarch	Role of an official in the Province of Asia.
augusti libertus	Status of a freedman of the Emperor.
auxilia	Non-legionary soldiers and units, both infantry and cavalry.
beneficiarius	Role of a soldier posted for special duties by a superior. Status: that of the officer making the appointment.
censitor	Role of a census official.
centurion	Role of a soldier commanding (i) a century [80 men] or (ii) auxiliary cohort.
civitas	A local government authority.
classis	A fleet.
cohors	One of ten units making up (i) a legion or (ii) an infantry unit of auxiliary troops.
colonia	A self-governing urban settlement.
comes	Role of (i) a senior official, or (ii) military commander in the later Empire.
commentariensis	Role of an office holder on the staff of a governor.
concilium provinciae	Provincial council. Role: mainly to maintain the imperial cult.
curator	Role of a manager.
dux	Role: a commander of troops in later Empire.
iuridicus	Role of a judicial officer, dispensing justice.
laticlavius	Word denoting senatorial rank.

latus clavus	Status of a man entitled to wear the broad stripe.
legatus augusti pro praetore	Role of the governor in an imperial province.
legatus legionis	Role: commanding officer of a legion.
libertus	Status of a freedman.
limes	The term for a frontier. The space between states.
magister	Role of a supervisor, governor, or office holder.
praeses	Role of a governor in the later Empire.
proconsul	Role of a governor of a senatorial province.
publican	Role of tax farmers, contracted to collect official taxes for the government. They were supervised by imperial procurators.
quaestor	Role: Junior magistrate. Status: senatorial rank.
res publica	A term for a government unit, sometimes used instead of civitas.
singularis	Role of a soldier with duties as guardsman.
tribe	A group of families claiming descent from an ancestor either by bloodline or adoption; having also a recognised leader (chief) and a common culture religion and dialect, and occupying a specific geographical area.
vicarius	Role of a supreme governor supervising a group of provinces.
vicus	A settlement outside a fort; sometimes called canabae. Vicani = a resident of a vicus.
vigiles	Role of magistrates responsible for the watch and security.
vir clarissimus	Most distinguished man. Status: senator.

vir egregious	A distinguished man. Status: junior procurator.
vir illustris	An illustrious man. Status: the highest ranking official in the later Empire.
vir perfectissimus	Most perfect man. Status: an equestrian official from the third century CE.
vir spectabilis	A notable man. Status of a high ranking official in the later Empire.

Definition of Administrative Terms:

accountability	A feature of a role relationship, in which a subordinate is obliged to account for his (her) work to a superior.
authority	The sanctioned right of the occupant of a role (i) to act as organisationally defined; (ii) to reward or punish subordinates; (iii) to have access to stated resources.
collateral relationship	The relationship between roles whose activities interact, and where neither role has authority over the other.
crossover role	A role where the occupant has authority which spans the roles of specified subordinates.
delegation	The giving of authority to a role occupant in order to meet defined objectives, and for which resources are allocated.
environment	That which provides resources to an organisation that are economic, political, social, legal, fiscal, physical, and cultural.
power	The personal ability and willingness to perform the activities of the role and use the allocation of people, money and materials for the achievement of stated objectives.

role	A set of expectations to be discharged through tasks placed on the occupant by a superior, who should indicate the objectives, activities and resources of the role.
role relationship	The defined condition between roles.
situation	(i) manifest: the situation as formally described; (ii) assumed: the situation as variously assumed by individuals in an organisation; (iii) extant: the situation as revealed by exploration, experience and analysis; (iv) requisite: the situation as it would have to be in order to meet a given context most appropriately.
staff role	A role occupant who assists a superior in supervising his (her) subordinates. The role may be specific to a certain area of activity, or it may be general. At a junior level the role may be as a personal assistant, where there is no authority to issue instructions.

INSCRIPTIONS ILLUSTRATIVE OF ROLES AND DUTIES IN PROVINCIAL ADMINISTRATION

Note

RIB = *Roman Inscriptions in Britain*, I. Richmond and R. P. Wright.

CIL = *Corpus of Latin Inscriptions (Corpus Inscriptionum Latinarum)*

Many inscriptions were set up in honour of an Emperor. The inscription dedicated to Claudius set up in Rome may be taken as typical of many.

> Tiberius Claudius Caesar Augustus Germanicus, son of Drusus: Pontifex Maximus, holder of the tribune's power 11 times, of the consulship 5 times, hailed as "Imperator" ... times [22 or 23], father of his country: erected by the senate and people of Rome because he received the submission of 11 kings of Britain, overthrown without any loss, and because he first brought barbarian tribes beyond the ocean into the dominion of the Roman people.
>
> *Inscriptiones Latinae Selectae*, H. Dessau, 216

Repeated declarations of loyalty to the Emperor were essential. Official greetings were sent by governors. Inscriptions were also erected by provincial councils, as in London (RIB 5).

> To the divine power of the emperor the province of Britain (set this up).

Sometimes an individual would set up an inscription on which his career was described, as in the case of Pliny the Younger. One such was placed at the baths of Como which Pliny had funded.

Gaius Plinius Caecilius, son of Lucius, a member of the Oufentina tribe, consul, augur, propraetorian legate with consular power appointed to the province of Pontus-Bithynia, by the emperor Caesar Nerva Trajan Augustus Germanicus Dacicus, father of his country, curator of the river Tiber's bed, banks, together with the sewers of the city; prefect of the Treasury of Saturn, prefect of the Military Treasury, praetor, tribune of the people, imperial quaestor, commissioner for the equestrians, military tribune in Legio III Gallica, magistrate on the Board of Ten dealing with lawsuits...

The inscription then goes on to list Pliny's bequests (*Documents illustrating the Principates of Nerva, Trajan and Hadrian*, E. M. Smallwood, Number 230).

Datable to early third century CE, a similar inscription from Caerwent reads:

To Tiberius Claudius Paulinus, the legate of the Second Legion Augusta, the proconsul of the province of Narbonensis, the propraetorian legate of the emperor for the province of Lugdunensis, this was erected by the decree of the council of the civitas of the Silures.

Paulinus' career, as stated here, shows how an official could move from a senatorial to an imperial province as well as from a military to an administrative command. Later he became governor of Britannia Secunda, the province having been divided between Prima and Secunda by Septimius Severus.

The inscription seems to indicate a viable relationship between the Silures and the local garrison commander. In the first century the tribe was regarded as one of the most warlike in Britain.

On other inscriptions the name of the governor follows the details of the Emperor to whom the inscription is dedicated, and before a statement of who erected it.

Imperator Titus Caesar Vespasian Augustus, son of the deified Vespasian, Pontifex Maximus, holder of the tribune's power 9 times, hailed as Imperator 15 times, seven times consul and nominated for an eighth consulship, censor, father of the fatherland; and Caesar Domitian, son of the deified Vespasian, six times consul and nominated for a seventh consulship, leader of youth and member of all the colleges of priests; Gnaeus Julius Agricola, Imperial Governor: the Borough of Verulamium to mark the building of the basilica.

Agricola may have had a good working relationship with Titus (*Britannia*, S. S. Frere, page 201).

Titus had a close emotional relationship with Berenice, who was of the house of Herod which provided a number of client kings for the provinces of the geographical area of Palestine.

> Queen Berenice, daughter of his majesty king Agrippa, and king Agrippa restored completely this [? Temple] built by king Herod their great-grandfather which had fallen down through age and adorned it with marble [pavements or statues] and six columns.
>
> *Select Documents of the Principates of the Flavian Emperors*, M. McCrum
> and A. G. Woodhead

Tombstones often give the role of the deceased, in this case one of the important procurators. A subordinate of the procurator also set up an inscription in Bath, where there could have been a branch office (RIB 179).

> To the spirits of the departed (and) of Gaius Julius Alpinus Classicianus, son of Gaius, of the Fabian voting tribe ... procurator of the province of Britain; Julia Pacata Indiana, daughter of Indus, his wife, had this built.
> London (RIB 12)

A law officer was in post, when needed, in some provinces, of which one was Britain.

> ... imperial juridical legate of the province of Britain on account of the Dacian victory.
>
> London (RIB 8)

A military officer could also have had responsibility for the supervision of an area, a duty which he combined with his military command, in this case a centurion who was also praepositus (commandant) of the region.

To ... for the welfare of our emperor Caesar Alexander Augustus and of Julia Mamaea the mother of our lord [the Emperor] and of the army under the charge of Valerius Crescens Fulvianus, propraetorian governor, Titus Floridius Natalis, legionary centurion and commandant of the unit and of the region, restored from ground-level and dedicated this temple from his own resources according to the reply of the god...

Ribchester (RIB 587)

The army units could be posted to non-military activities; working at a quarry in Cumbria, for example.

A detachment of the Second Legion Augusta; the working-face of Apr(...) under Agricola, optio.
[An optio was a subordinate aide to a centurion]

Lower Gelt Bridge (RIB 1008)

Even sailors could be sent on naval duties. Here a detachment of the Classis Britannica, the British fleet, whose main base was at Boulogne, were engaged on building work at Condercum (the fort at Benwell, Northumberland).

For the emperor Caesar Trajan Hadrian Augustus under Aulus Platorius Nepos, emperor's propraetorian governor, the detachment of the British fleet [built this].

Benwell (RIB 1340)

There are numerous inscriptions erected by soldiers on detached duty, for example as a speculator, a scout or messenger on the governor's staff based at the provincial headquarters (RIB 122: speculator legionis), or as a soldier in charge of the horses at a governor's headquarters (strator consularis). RIB 233 is interesting because the inscription was found at Irchester, Northants, where the dedicator set up the inscription as sacred to the departed spirits, but making the memorial to himself. Yet another was stationed with the governor's bodyguard with the title of eques singularis. Beneficiarii could be found at numerous sites, where a governor or other official had sent them for some particular purpose, for example at Winchester (RIB 88) and Dorchester (RIB 235). These inscriptions generally state no more than:

1) to whom the inscription is dedicated, usually a god or in memory of someone
2) the name of the dedicator
3) his role or position

There are inscriptions set up by the council of a civitas or other urban unit, for example

> For the emperor Caesar Marcus Aurelius Numerianus the civitas of the Dobunni ... (set this up).
>
> Kenchester (RIB 2250)

The Emperor is honoured, but the rest of the text may indicate the frontier of the Dobunni.

A decurion, a councillor of the civitas for some purpose or a relative or friend might mention his status on his tombstone.

> To the spirits of the departed, Volusia Faustina, a citizen of Lindum [Lincoln] lived 26 years 1 month and 26 days, Senecio, a councillor, set this up [in remembrance] of his wife, who deserved this commemoration.
>
> Lincoln (RIB 250)

At Bath we read of an unknown councillor who lived to be 80 (RIB 141).

Even a small village might hold a collection to pay for an honorific inscription.

> To Jupiter, best and greatest, and to Vulkanus, for the welfare of our own lord Marcus Antonius Gordianus Pius Felix Augustus, the headmen of the villagers dedicated this altar, from money contributed by the villagers.
>
> Old Carlisle (RIB 899)

After the reforms of Diocletian, the title of governor changed from legatus augusti pro praetore to praeses, who was addressed as *vir perfectissimus*, a most perfect man.

> To Jupiter, the best and greatest, the most perfect Lucius Septimius ... governor of Britannia Prima and a citizen of Reims restored this monument.

Appendix

At the back of the monument is a further inscription:

> This statue and column were erected under the old religion. Septimius, the ruler of Britannia Prima restores.
>
> Cirencester (RIB 103)

It seems likely that the texts date from some time after the Edict of Milan (313 CE), which promoted Christianity. During his short reign (360–363 CE), Julian attempted to restore the old religion.

FURTHER READING

Introduction
For a deeper understanding of organisation analysis, A. D. Newman, *Organisation Analysis*, 1973, and E. Jaques, *A General Theory of Bureaucracy*, 1976, will be found useful.

Chapter 1: Boundaries of Empire
A good historical atlas is always an asset. Gibbon's tour of the Empire in *The Decline and Fall*, volume 1, is still serviceable.

Chapter 2: Romanitas
J. Liversidge, *Daily Life in the Roman Empire*, 1976; J. Carcopino, *Daily Life in Ancient Rome*, first published in 1941 but with many reprints; D. Dudley, *Roman Society*, 1970; and N. Lewis, *Life in Egypt under Roman Rule*, 1983, can be used as starting points, to be followed by the numerous studies of individual provinces.

There are textbooks on law: B. Nicholas, *An Introduction to Roman Law*, 1962, describes the system.

Bowman, *Life and Letters on the Roman Frontier*, 1944, throws light on the use of colloquial Latin. It should be read alongside A. R. Birley, *Garrison Life at Vindolanda*, 2002, and M. Millett, *The Romanization of Britain*, 1990. Thereafter, the reader will find books on most topics touching on *Romanitas*.

Chapter 3: Central Government; Chapter 4: The Governor in Office; Chapter 5: The Procurator
A. R. Birley, *The Roman Government of Britain*, 2005, is invaluable for these chapters, to which may be added his translation and edition of Tacitus, *The Agricola*, 1999. H. F. Jolowicz, *Historical Introduction to the Study of Roman Law*, 1965, has sections dealing with these subjects.

Chapter 6: Client Kings
Again, A. R. Birley, *The Roman Government of Britain*, is helpful. To this may be added M. Goodman, *Rome and Jerusalem*, 2007; and though it is fairly old (1932), W. Oesterley & T. Robinson, *A History of Israel*, vol. 2 still has its merits. The Christian New Testament also throws light on the rule of Herod and his family. However, the Gospels are not biographies and The Acts of the Apostles has a distinctive narrative. Nonetheless, something of the nature of client kingship can be discerned. Herod and his family seemed to find particular favour with the ruling house: e.g., it is possible that the centurion at Capernaum was stationed there having been posted to Agrippa.

Chapter 7: Egypt
Lewis, quoted above, may be enough to start the reader into further studies.
P. Oxy. = Papyri Oxyrhynchus

Chapter 8: Local Government
A. R. Birley, quoted above, is invaluable. M. Beard, *Pompeii*, 2008; A. Butterworth & R. Laurence, *Pompeii*, 2005.

Chapter 9: The Roman Army
G. Webster, *The Roman Imperial Army*, 3rd edition, 1985; and Y. Le Bohec, *The Imperial Roman Army*, English edition, 1994.

Postscript
J. McManners (ed.), *The Oxford History of Christianity*, 1990; D. MacCulloch, *A History of Christianity*, 2009; J. Herrin, *The Formation of Christendom*, 1987; C. Wickham, *The Inheritance of Rome*, 2009; P. Heather, *The Fall of the Roman Empire*, 2005.

General

J. Richardson, *Roman Provincial Administration*, 1976; J. Rogan, *Reading Roman Inscriptions*, 2006. The latter has chapters dealing with inscriptions relevant to chapters 3, 4, 5, 6, 8 and 9 above.

The Roman Society houses material covering all the subjects of this volume, and the reader can be kept up to date by subscribing to membership; and the same may be said of the catalogues of Amberley Publishing.

INDEX